CLIMB 'TIL YOUR DREAMS COME TRUE

A Book of Family, Faith and Love

LILY AILENE DECK

CLIMB 'TIL YOUR DREAMS COME TRUE

A Book of Family, Faith and Love

LILY AILENE DECK

Editing: Lon and Trudy Brunk
Cover design: Judy Sery
Book designe: Judy Sery

ISBN: 979-8814193995

CLIMB 'TIL YOUR DREAMS COME TRUE

A Book of Family, Faith and Love

LILY AILENE DECK

Acknowledgements

This is a book of love. Ever since I was a little girl, I have had a great desire to inform people about the life and times of my wonderful family. I want to thank all my family and friends, past and present, for being part of my life and part of this book. Without your love and encouragement, I could not put my deep feelings into this format. I am so blessed to believe in Jesus, and I always give thanks to Him for this life and this family.

My husband, Arnold Deck, loved researching family histories and I am indebted to him for being my husband and my partner in life. Although he has passed away, Arnold left many legacies including our beautiful children.

I could never have completed this project without the assistance of Lon Brunk and his lovely wife, Trudy Brunk. Lon is the son of my brother George (Gee Gee to me), and his family has resided in Anaheim, California for many years. Lon and Trudy have lived an interesting life and are well-educated especially in the technology field. They used those skills to merge and edit all the documents and publish the completed book online.

My granddaughter, Chelsea Hicks, was an immense help in working with Lon and Trudy to send versions and drafts of this book over the Internet. We kept the phone, mail, email, and copy centers busy throughout the process of completing this book.

This book is nonfiction except for two stories I took the liberty to write which I call, "Inspirational Novelettes." The two novelettes are partly true. The titles are, "Golden Ribbon" and "Terror on a Thirteenth Halloween."

"Climb 'Til Your Dreams Come True"

Often your tasks will be many,
And more than you think you can do.
Often the road will be rugged
And the hills insurmountable, too.

But always remember, the hills ahead
Are never as steep as they seem,
And with *Faith* in your heart start upward
And climb 'Til you reach your dream.

For nothing in life that is worthy
Is never too hard to achieve
If you have the courage to try it
And you have the Faith to believe.

For *Faith* is a force that is greater
Than knowledge or power or skill
And many defeats turn to triumph
If you trust in God's wisdom and will.

For *Faith* is a mover of mountains.
There's nothing that God cannot do,
So start out today with Faith in your heart
And *'Climb 'Til Your Dream Comes True'!*

- Helen Steiner Rice

...If thou canst believe, all things are possible
to him that believeth.

- Mark 9:23

Table of Contents

"MEMORIES OF A WONDERFUL PLACE"

Have you ever known of a place, be it house, cabin or land, that you wonder why so many people throughout their lives love to go there just to sit on the beautiful wrap-around porch in their lovely rocking chairs and old-fashioned swings and reminisce about by-gone days, events, relatives and anything else that comes to mind?

Some cannot get the time or means to go there, but they love to talk about that wonderful place to others or take a mini-vacation mentally and enjoy strolling down that memory lane. Such is my maternal grandfather and grandmother's home in West Virginia.

THE PITTMAN HOME: THE GRAND HOUSE IN BECKLEY, W. VA.

Sitting on a prominent hill in the pretty town of Beckley, West Virginia, which lies in the southern part of the state, is the beautiful home which belonged to my grandfather and grandmother, George Marvin Pittman, and Martha Ann Meadows Pittman. The house itself was a grand one considering the times in which they lived. Cousins and aunts told me the story of how grandfather wanted a big Grand House to present to his lovely bride. Their plan was to have a large family, which they eventually did. They were forward looking people and raised to be industrious, independent, and possessing a lot of faith in their God and the future.

I recently read the deed to that house and land written by a prominent Beckley attorney. The deed came to me through the gracious act of one of my favorite cousins who lived in the Grand House while growing up. I owe a debt of gratitude to my cousin, Betty Bostick Williams, who now lives in Elyria, Ohio. You will hear about her later in this book. They signed the deed on April 10, 1913.

Grandfather bought the house with a large area of land where the grown-up children could build houses for their future families. Most noticeable was the high hill with surrounding level lots with plenty of room for a huge yard, big, tall trees, both evergreens and deciduous varieties and space for a large garden. He could see, in his mind's eye, his large new lot complete with the outbuildings such as cellars and workshops, a barn, and a blacksmith shop. Grandfather would see his beautiful vision come true, in fact, the attorney referred to the house in the deed as a "mansion house." My grandparents did everything they could do to make sure it became a "mansion home" for the whole family.

Grandfather purchased the "mansion house" from Mr. J. W. Harper and his wife, Laura, for the sum of three thousand, five hundred dollars ($3,500). As stated in the deed, grandfather paid a down payment of three hundred dollars ($300) that day, April 10, 1913. He paid the remaining $3200 in annual installments on that same date each year plus the annual interest rate of 6% per annum. The contract was for ten years, so every year on April 10, Grandfather paid the $300 plus the interest of $18 per year. His last payment was on April 10, 1923.

Grandfather was a fine Christian as was my Grandmother. Grandfather was one of the founders of the Church of the Nazarene on Johnstown Road in Beckley. The church remains active to this day. He also helped to start the Sunset Memorial Park Cemetery on Harper Road in Beckley. He purchased the first four burial plots there for $280 and would later purchase other plots in the Sunset Memorial Park. Both of my grandparents died on the 31st of March; my grandmother died in 1938 and grandfather passed in 1949. My mother, Lillian Pittman Brunk, is buried near them as is my uncle Ronald Pittman who died at the age of twenty-one.

To me, the most beautiful thing in the house was the shiny cherry wood banisters leading from the first floor to the second floor. The shiny banisters were easy on the grandkids' bottoms as we slid down them. Even though this was forbidden by the parents and grandparents, when the opportunity presented itself, what little one could resist? We would just as soon have a spanking as to not enjoy that wonderful ride!

That beautiful stairway led from the downstairs halls to a landing at the second floor. It curved around to the hallways where the five bedrooms were located. I often imagined as I climbed those stairs that if I kept climbing in my life, I would eventually see my mother at Heaven's Gate.

Downstairs there were two bedrooms. Each room had a fireplace in it because in the early days of the century that was the only way to heat each room. I remember the beautifully scrolled woodwork of each mantle over the fireplace. No two mantles were alike because they were hand made.

Grandpa had the bedroom to the right of the big parlor. This room had seven circular windows in a semi-circle. He had a tall chifforobe and he kept goodies for the children in one of the top drawers where we could not reach them. I remember him giving me sticks of gum and peanuts.

At the end of one of the long hallways on the main floor, was my Aunt Mattie and Uncle Herman Bostick's bedroom. Aunt Mattie was mother's sister who lived over on the next hill before she came to live with Grandpa. After Grandmother passed in 1938, Grandpa could not keep up with all the work, so Aunt Mattie and her whole family came to live with Grandpa to do the work. Aunt Mattie, Uncle Herman, son Ray, daughter Betty and the twins, Marvin, and Melvin, moved in with Grandpa.

There was plenty of arduous work to do including cows, horses, and chickens to feed, plus gardens to tend. I am not sure if they had any pigs at the time. Aunt Mattie did the housework. She was one of my favorite aunts. She and mother were in the first bunch of five children. There were four boys and seven girls for a total of eleven children.

Upstairs in the Grand House there were five bedrooms along two L-shaped hallways. As the children grew up and married, Grandpa set aside two upstairs bedrooms where the young couple could start with their housekeeping. Grandpa did not charge them any rent. One room was the kitchen, dining area and the other room was the bedroom. I remember Aunt Macil and Uncle Roy living there at one time with their girls, Dorothy, and Joy.

At the end of one of the long hallways upstairs, there was a large window. We could easily climb out of that window onto the top of the front porch. We would take blankets, pillows, and snacks out so we could lie down and look at the stars. We could also see more down to earth activities like the goings-on downtown.

During the summer months, the carnival would come to town and locate in the large area near Waterdale Swimming Pool. If we had any money at all, we would go down and enjoy a few rides and the magic of the travelling carnival. Carnivals were a welcome relief from the daily work and brought the outside world to our little community in West Virginia.

As already stated, our cousin Betty lived in the Grand House and was the most mischievous one among us. She and the cousins would shimmy down from the top of the porch and slip down the hill, then sneak into the carnival.

Cousins Sissy and Faye lived across the lane on part of Grandpa's land. Their parents were my mother's brother, Uncle Harvey Pittman, his wife Gertrude and four children, Danny and Skitter (Rebecca), Margaret (Sissy) and Faye. Danny and Betty's older brother Ray were friends and often played music together. I remember their beautiful Hawaiian guitar and hearing such wonderful music.

One other cousin, Susie Teel, was the daughter of Mother's sister Aunt Laura and Uncle Quince Teel. Susie was a little older than Betty and Patty. There was not a lot of difference in the ages of the five girls, but I was always the tag-a-long.

The Pittman family has a reunion every year in Beckley, West Virginia. People gather from everywhere on the last Saturday in July. Over one hundred people attend from family members who live locally and those who travelled across the country to meet their relatives, learn about the family, and create new memories.

At one of the reunions, Betty told me she loved my sister Patty so much that she asked her father and mother if they would adopt Patty as her sister. They made this request on December 14, 1940, just one day after our mother died. Betty said it was fine with her parents, but our Daddy would not agree to the arrangement. He never wanted to see us separated. I suppose that is why we both ended up living with Daddy's sister, Aunt Maggie, in Pax, WV. Those were not good years for Patty and me. We were afraid of Aunt Maggie and whipped for our transgressions during the five or six years we were there. More about that in later chapters.

We never lived in the Grand House, but we visited there occasionally. It was always so wonderful to go there.

Grandpa's beautiful home holds so many fond memories for all their children (eleven in all) and all us grandchildren. Every room is special. And all the Pittman relatives feel that special feeling about Grandpa's house.

Marvin was the final family member to live there. The property was willed to him by his mother and father. After he passed, Gloria remained there for a year or two. The stained-glass windows, the antiques in the house, Marvin's tools and finally the house and the land were sold. What a sad day that was for the family. I heard that a female doctor and her businessman husband bought it and live there.

The only place in Grandpa's house that brings a pain to my heart is the big parlor with the beautiful stained-glass windows; because my beautiful, loving, gentle Mother lay there, so lovely, and still, just a few days before Christmas, in 1940. And I was not thinking of Christmas. All I could think about was how I wished Mother could move and put her arms around me for another hug.

THE ANCESTRY OF LILLIAN PITTMAN BRUNK

GEORGE AND MARTHA PITTMAN

My sisters and I have written our memories in this book, but I would like to include some of the genealogical information which I have gathered concerning my mother's lineage.

During the fall of 1987 and spring of 1988, my husband and I became interested in family trees and genealogy. He authored a book for The Church of the Brethren and then started on his family and mine. I am indebted to him for his perseverance in attempting a monumental task. He worked hours, even months taking pictures and including them in this book. Virtually all the pictures you enjoy are due to his scouting all over the area to obtain them and copy them.

While working on the Meadows Oil Inheritance ancestral lineage of our families, I obtained much valuable information about my family roots. I am indebted to Bob and Melba Underwood for helping us locate this information. Also, I am indebted to Jim Richardson from Charleston for helping me locate information in the Archives in Charleston. Now I will share with you what I can, so that you will know a little more about our roots.

It is difficult for an amateur writer to know what method to use in conveying his or her information. I have chosen to simply list the ancestral line and then to expound upon that. The following picture comes from our Pittman Family Reunion in 2016 and shows the descendants of George and Martha Pittman. There are additional photos of the reunions and family members in the Appendix.

2nd child

HARVEY
2/21/1894 - 2/20/1953
Gertrude

GEORGE
10/27/1869 - 3/31/1949

Martha Meadows Pittman
3/15/1867-3/31/1938

1st child

Laura Mae Teel
(Quince)
5/12/1892-6/26/74

8th child died when 21 years old

RONALD
5/2/1908 - 11-7-1929

3rd child

Lottie Cole
(Frederick)
6/27/1896-7/1/1983

The Martha Meadows and George Pittman family reunion

July 30 2016

Mark this day on your calendars. This reunion is always the last Saturday in July.

It will be held at Dry-Hill Prosperity Community Park

Please try to arrive between 11-11:30 AM to get lunch prepared by 12:30

Please bring dishes ready to serve. Meat will be provided.

This year we will *try* to have scheduled events so everyone can enjoy:

Lunch until 2

Auction until 3

Horseshoes and other activities until ?

Scott Pittman will take care of the activities

Please bring games for children

Please notify any others of this event

This year we will have karaoke.

10th child

DONALD
5/17/1914 - 8-28-1973
Irene

5th child

Lillian Brunk
(Sidney)
6/10/1902-12/13/1940

6th child

JACK
7/20/1904 - 2/4/1966

4th child

Maycel Brunk
(Roy)
10/16/1898-5/1/1980

11th child

Dorothy Mullins
(Winfred)

7th child

Mattie Bostick
(Herman)

9th child

Ruth Worley

THE PITTMAN REUNION 2016
(REUNIONS ARE HELD ON LAST SATURDAY IN JULY)

"THE MOST UNFORGETTABLE CHARACTER I EVER KNEW"

By Iris Yvonne (Brunk) Stover (Daughter)

Lillian Pittman Brunk

She won no medals; she had no titles; her name was never on the social register. And yet, she was one of the most unforgettable people I will ever know. All children instinctively loved her. She was friend, lecturer, confidant, disciplinarian, but, most of all, she was my mother.

It was in the 1930's and times were hard. Everyone was going through unusually demanding times following The Crash of 1929. The lot of the coal miner was never easy and was particularly difficult at the time. There were men who were in the process of trying to better the lot of the working man, and its birth pains of the coming industrial unions were beginning to be felt.

We lived in a small mining community in West Virginia. Our father worked from daylight until dark when there was any work. He averaged working two days per week. In season, our main supply of food came from a vegetable garden, supplemented by eggs from a few chickens (which every family had).

Through all these times, including a family of six children, my mother was a tower of strength. Her patience was momentous, her love next to the love of God. I realize, now, that when times were the worst, she smiled and loved us the most.

Oh, that there were more uncomplaining mothers with that special love that no one else has! Her greatest weapon was the quotation," *I trust you. I know you can do better. Won't you try for me?"* I would have moved mountains for her -- my greatest punishment was knowing I had disappointed her!

One Christmas, I recall, was particularly rough. Our father was gone, and it looked like this would be one Christmas we would not have a tree. I will never forget the way Mother looked as she said, "When you come home from school, there will be a tree for you." While we were gone, from somewhere, she gathered the trunk of a discarded tree with branches on it. She found a pine branch here and there that had been trimmed from other trees and thrown away.

When we came home, there stood the most beautiful tree I have ever had for Christmas. She had spent the entire day taping the branches on! How much fun we had trimming it with popcorn balls, paper chains, and odds and ends of tinsel and Christmas ornaments.

How gay, modest, old fashioned and lovable she was! She was ill and soon her wonderful life would be over. It was my sixteenth birthday. On this night, the moon was full. Nowhere in the world is there a scene more beautiful than in the hills of West Virginia as it rises over the hills and shines as a pathway through the valleys. I had gone for a walk with my boyfriend, and when we came back, she had set the table on our front lawn and the moonlight was our candles. The mountains were our scenery. The magic was indescribable. That Happy Birthday song still rings in my heart now as I remember how we sat around the table and sang.

How I used to feel sorry for the children who did not have a mother such as mine. Everyone in the village was poor, compared to our family. Sorry, that I did not have a car? A closet full of clothes? The popularity of the crowd? I was reared in the cradle of love and raised in the wisdom of Solomon! Poor? No! I wish my riches on every misguided youngster who cannot come banging through the door yelling, "Mom, I'm home! What's for supper?" Sorry I live in the state of West Virginia? The most *misunderstood and maligned state in the United States.* This scripture comes to me as I think of those by-gone days:" I *will lift up mine eyes to the hills from whence cometh my help? My help cometh from God, who made motherhood the most blessed estate in the world."*

Written by Yvonne Stover as a tribute to her mother. (Yvonne was 19 years old when her mother Lillian Pittman Brunk died.)

MOTHER AND DADDY MARRIED NOVEMBER 16, 1919

Beckley First Baptist Church

SYDNEY AND LILIAN BRUNK

Mother was born in a small country community named Central between Oak Hill and Fayetteville in Fayette County, West Virginia. She was born on June 10, 1902, to my maternal grandparents George Marvin Pittman and Martha Ann Meadows Pittman. They named her "Lillian," but everyone called her "Lelia." She was Grandpa and Grandma Pittman's fifth child from a total of eleven children, seven girls and four boys.

Mother was a beautiful lady everyone told me. I do know she had sparkling beautiful brown eyes and was tall at five feet six inches in height. She had beautiful chestnut brown hair. She was a very patient, genteel person who loved nature, God, children, and all people.

Daddy was the last child born to John Griffith Brunk and Nancy Margaret Clemens Brunk. Altogether, there were twelve children in the Brunk family. Daddy was introduced to mother by her sister Macil Pittman and Daddy's brother Roy (James Royal Brunk). I have seen a picture of the four of them on a picnic. Daddy was 5-feet 10-inches tall, and he was handsome. He had black hair and blue eyes.

Daddy was born in a small coal town in the beautiful and famous New River Gorge, West Virginia. He only had an eighth-grade education, but was a very inventive and intelligent person, as was my mother. Daddy was born on August 15, 1897. They both loved to read so they were self-educated. I am sure they were a handsome couple. They set up housekeeping in a house on Sprague Hill which may have been part of Grandpa Pittman's property.

They were married in a nice big church, the First Baptist on Neville Street in Beckley, WV. I think it must have been mother's church since she was a Baptist. They took us to a Presbyterian Church when we were living at Brooklyn, WV. Yvonne was born in the house in Sprague and was their first child.

Daddy and Mother were blessed to have their children born in a certain order. First, Yvonne was born on May 30, 1921. Her name was Iris Yvonne. Next, Ruth Wilma was born January 8th, 1923, so there was less than two years between them. George Griffith, who was named after both of his grandfathers, George Pittman, and John Griffith Brunk and we all called him Gee Gee. He was born July 3rd, 1925. Paul Sidney was born April 9th, 1927.

There was a longer period between Paul and Patty. Patricia Ann was born June 23rd, 1933. So, there were six years and two months between Paul and Patty. Daddy and mother made the move from northern West Virginia to southern West Virginia during those years, due to scarcity of jobs up North and a coal mining bust going on in the southern West Virginia region. Then from June 23, 1933, until October 28, 1935, along came the 6th and final child of the Sidney/Lillian pair. So that meant two years and four months between Patty and me, Lily Ailene. The children coming in pairs worked out good for Mother and Daddy. They wanted each pair of children to be close and helpful to each other. And so, it was!

Mother and Daddy held Yvonne back a year in school so that she and Wilma could go to school together. They even graduated the same year from Pax high school. They did the same thing with Gee Gee and Paul. But when it got down to Patty and me, the school board had something to say about the plan. So, we could not pal along together at school.

Patty was two years ahead of me. But throughout our lives that togetherness held. There was an influence that caused us to be remarkably close to each other. But I want to make it clear that we all, as a family, are close even when the family broke apart due to Mother's death. We have remained a close family, though we have scattered to the four corners of the United States. We always have, and we always will be close in life and in death.

But now we know why Patty was not adopted and did not become Betty's sister. Daddy wanted Patty and me to grow up together. And we did for a while, six years to be exact.

A few years ago, I went to the First Baptist Church in Beckley on a Sunday morning just because I wanted to know more about the place where Daddy and Mother were married. It is a big church and is still active. I read somewhere that mother was a Baptist, so this was her church that she had been attending.

The church had a big choir, piano, and organ and one of my favorites, a Hand Bell Choir. After the music, the Pastor introduced me to the congregation. He told them mother had attended there years ago and my parents were married there in 1919.

When they were married, mother was seventeen and Daddy was twenty-two years old. I don't have a picture of their wedding. Families took very few pictures in those days. But I do have a picture of Aunt Macil, mother's sister, and Uncle Roy when they were on a picnic. Mother and Daddy were introduced to each other by Aunt Macil and Uncle Roy. Back then, a brother or sister would introduce a sibling to prospective dates since there were so few people then. The children of the two couples were double first cousins (kin on both sides of the family). Macil and Roy had two daughters, Dorothy, and Joy. We have always been close but now both have died. Joy's daughter, Barbara Jo Byrd and I call each other every week or two. Barbara Jo says my home feels like HOME now that Grandpa's house is no longer in the family.

MEMORIES

How to begin? The sweet fragrance from the lilacs in the vase on my dining room table waft across the room to where I sit with pen in hand. That fragrance fills me with remembrances. Somewhere in my childhood, lilacs must have held a prominent position. The sweet fragrance and temporary existence of my mother and dad are just like lilacs. So, brief. So fragrant.

MOTHER: LILLIAN (LELIA) PITTMAN BRUNK

I turned five on October 28, 1940. Mother died that same year on Friday, the 13th of December.

Mother, I don't have very many memories of you. I will relate the sad ones first to get those out of the way, so I can leave you with the good ones I have:

I remember:

Climbing up on the bed when you were sick. Someone told me to get down. That hurt because I wanted to be near you. But I never told anyone about it hurting. I just could not understand.

The funeral. Two men argued as to whether I could go to see you. One of them lifted me up. You were so beautiful. Beautiful dark hair and a beautifully shaped face. Your dress was either pink or blue. Pink, I think. The funeral was held at Grandpa Pittman's *big, beautiful, two-story house* up on the hill at Sprague, West Virginia. I sat near the front on the first row, I believe. I had on a new pink dress, pink socks and white shoes bought for me by my Uncle Guy, I think.

I remember standing upstairs by the window, watching as they placed the casket in the hearse. The cars all filed in behind, and then they wound their way down the hill. It seems, in my mind's eye that it was raining. I don't really know. It was only raining in my heart. I felt lost and deserted. I have always remembered feeling like I had dwindled in size to a grain of sand in a big open space.

You are sitting at Grandpa's organ playing music and I loved it! That is somehow related to the haunting melody I sometimes hear in my heart. It gives me a strange, nostalgic feeling in which happiness and sadness all intertwined together and I think of you and Dad and us kids and the small log house up in Brunk Hollow.

Hearing Daddy's car coming up the dirt road through the woods, I had a feeling of excitement. Daddy, you, Patty, and I, lounging on a quilt beside the house. Supper was over. Daddy was reading the newspaper. The small kitchen from which good smells radiated. The oven door was down and there was a skillet of cornbread sitting there. Brown beans were simmering in a big pot on the back of the stove. They smelled yummy and made my mouth water.

Patty and I drinking water from the spring - dog fashion. It was the best tasting water anywhere!

You are throwing scraps to the chickens. We had names for all of them. Our dog, Rex followed closely on your heels.

You are washing clothes on the back porch, with the old gasoline-powered washer going "bang, bang." Patty and I were sliding down a steep bank covered with pine needles, under a big old pine near the road. We could hear the washer pounding away. We both wore out our panties!

Discovering Paul and Gee Gee's cave as we walked out the path around the hill, near the creek. We found pans and skillets there and the remains of their campfire. The boys told us if we told, a bear would get us. We told you and you didn't seem a bit upset. You said, "That is all right. They need some things for cooking." When I went back there years later, and the house was empty and deteriorating, I walked up to that cave, and there were those old rusty pans, still there, after decades of time had passed. I had a feeling you always understood your children and our needs. I know you really loved us with a very deep love. Your rose bushes and shrubs and pine tree were still there. It made me feel your spirit there because I knew your gentle hands had planted them. I touched them tenderly and felt your nearness.

A moonlit night- the smell of roses in the air. We had a

small table outside in the yard beside the pine tree. It was a beautiful evening filled with starlight. A tablecloth was on the table. Roses were in a vase or glass on the table. Several of us were having a party. It was someone's birthday - yours since yours is June 10th. We were making a memory that night. My favorite memory of you, Mom.

"Mom, we miss you, but the time when we will see you again is drawing nearer. Until then, I thank God for my brief, fragrant memories of you. You are the reason I love moonlight and roses (and tea) so well.

SIDNEY DANIEL BRUNK

AILENE, SIDNEY WITH
GRANDSON DAVID BRUNK

I remember Daddy...

"Daddy, I knew you longer than Mom, but though you lived 15 years longer than she, I didn't see you all that much. We were only with you a short while when you began your wanderings. But I do remember...

The Christmas you bought us everything a little girl's heart could desire. Patty and I received a play sewing machine, a table and chair set, dishes, dolls, and other goodies. Patty and I lived with Mother's sisters, Lottie, and Macil for a while, then went to live with Aunt Maggie for about 5 years. You came there many times to see us and one time you brought us new dolls. I named mine Marguerite. I have postcards that are post-marked from Wilmington, Delaware and Fort Myers, Florida. I went to live with Yvonne and Jerry when I was 11 years old and stayed there until I married at the age of twenty. Nine great years! Patty lived with Wilma and Herbert those years. We had a wonderful life with our sisters and their families.

I remember you driving the 1936 model Ford up Dry Hill Road to Beckley. You sang all the way. Patty and I joined in often. You taught Patty and me how to sing soprano, alto and tenor when we were young (less than 7 and 5 years of age.) We could sing trio numbers at a tender age and the three of us could switch parts. I have often thanked you for this legacy. I remember the three of us singing, "Beautiful, Beautiful Texas, Where the Beautiful Bluebonnets Grow," "Life Is Like a Mountain Railroad," and my favorite "Red Sails in The Sunset." You whistled, too.

Daddy, I remember...

You took Patty and me for a walk in the woods near the creek by our cabin near Pax, WV. You cut off chunks of bark from a tree and we used spoons, scraped the inside of the bark, and ate it. It was sweet and good.

You got up one night and gave me a dose of (I think) kerosene and sugar for the croup. I hated it, but you said it would make me better, so I took the awful stuff, and you gave me a big hug. I felt loved. You tucked me into my beautiful cherry wood bed.

You caught Patty and me sliding down the banister and took off your belt and gave us a whipping. Then I saw a look of pain or guilt or something in your eyes, and you lay on the bed and took us up on the bed and gave us a big hug. I had a feeling you really didn't want to whip us in the first place.

You and the boys were up on top of the hill hoeing corn. I

was carrying water to you up the hill. I almost stepped on a big black snake. You killed it and held it up to Gee Gee to measure its length. It was six feet long!

You got off the train at the Prince (WV) station. It was time for my graduation from high school. When you got off the train, you had a cane, and you were limping. Your left arm and leg were paralyzed from the brain tumor. You looked so vulnerable. I wanted to cry. Your surgery had lasted for around 12 hours. They had lifted off the top of your skull to try to rid you of the cancer. But I was so happy and proud that you had come in to see me graduate.

When you came to visit us at Crab Orchard, WV. You had ridden the bus and were walking down the path, down the hill to the house. You fell and I ran up the hill to meet you. I helped you up. You smelled of alcohol. I said, "Daddy, why do you do this to us, and to yourself?" You began to cry and said, "Ailene, there has never been a day since Lelia died that I don't miss her." We stood there and cried together. That was the day I understood why.

Daddy, we will meet again someday. Thank you, Daddy, for memories. Thank you, God, for lilacs.

I

Sidney Daniel Brunk's Ancestor's

Written by his youngest daughter, Ailene Brunk Deck

Brief Outline of Sidney's family tree:

Sidney Daniel Brunk - Born August 15, 1895 at Demock, Fayette County, West Virginia
Married Lillian (Lelia) Pittman on Nov. 16, 1919 at the
    First Baptist Church, Neville St. Beckley, Raleigh County,WV
Died Dec. 14 (shortly after midnight) 1955 at Wilmington, Delaware
Buried at Pax Community Cemetery, Pax, Fayette Co. WV
Children: Iris Yvonne, Ruth Wilma, George Griffeth, Paul Sidney
                            Patricia Ann, Lily Ailene

Sidney's Father:
John Griffeth Brunk Born: April 27, 1852 at Montgomery Co. Virginia
Married: Nancy Margaret Clemens on Dec. 24, 1874 at Blacksburg,Va
    (Nancy Margaret's Family Geneology appears later in
    this book) This information from Family Bible.
    They were married at the home of her parents, William
    and Harriet Price Clemens, Blacksburg, Va. on
    Dec. 24, 1874 by S.R. Smith. To this union was born
    12 Children. Nancy and John G. lived in the Pric's
    Fork, and Blacksburg area and later moved to Bolt, WV.
    They again moved to Fayette County at Pax.
Died: John Griffeth died April, 1933 at Pax,WV.
Buried: Pax Community Cemetery, Pax, Fayette Co. WV.
Children: John G. & Nancy Margaret were the parents of 12
    children.
Parents: John Griffeth was the 6th child born
    to Jacob Brunk and Elizabeth (Betsy) Keffer.
Note: For more information see Page 97 of Ivan Brunk's book
    entitled JACOB'S LADDER available through the author
    at 3421 Montilla Court, Sarasota, Florida 33582.

Jacob Brunk - Born: Sept. 24, 1819 Montogomery Co.Va.
Married: June 7 or 8, 1841, Montgomery Co. Va.
    ELIZABETH (BETSY) KEFFER was born May 2, 1819 in Va.
    and died in 1900; she was buried in Blacksburg, Va;
    she was the daughter of George and Ruth Keffer.
Died: Jacob died 1853 in Roanoke Co. Va

Children: 6 children were born to Jacob and Elizabeth:
    1 George 2 Nancy 3 Hannah 4 Christopher 5 William
    6 Griffeth
Note: Many thanks to Ivan Brunk for the information about
    Jacob and Elizabeth: See pg 85 of his book entitled
    JACOB'S LADDER.
Parents: JACOB BRUNK AND NANCY SHANK

Jacob Brunk - Born: Oct. 11, 1784 in Maryland
Married:NANCY SHANK Oct. 10, 1806, Botetourt Co. Va.
    Nancy was born 1786 in Pennsylvania. She was the
    daughter of Christian Shank
Died: Nov. 8, 1969
Buried: Beard Cemetery, Roanoke Co. Va. (According to Ivan
    Brunk in his book, JACOB'S LADDER P. 202, Jacob's

FAMILY MEMORIES

RUTH, MATTIE, LILLIAN AND
DOROTHY PITTMAN

I remember...

Yvonne taking Patty and me for a walk down the road. There was a path with a large, moss-covered rock, where we sat while Yvonne sang songs to us. She sang one which I love, called "Red Sails in The Sunset," also one entitled "Somewhere Over the Rainbow." I had a peaceful, tranquil feeling. There was a big, hollow tree where we played hide-and-seek.

Wilma, wrapping Patty and myself in winter-wear and taking

us down to the frozen creek where she pulled us up and down the creek, using the clothes line pole for us to hold on to. What fun!

Mother, helping us make snow ice-cream. It tasted yummy!

Yvonne, sitting in the creek, reading a book, while the sparkling, clear water rushed over her legs.

Gee Gee always feeling like a heating stove when he was in bed! Once, when I had the croup, I climbed in bed and snuggled next to him. The next morning, someone asked me why I liked to get in his bed, and I replied, "He's so warm. I feel like I'm next to the stove!" Our brother Gee Gee was the main farm hand when Daddy was at work.

Paul, jumping off a big rock into the creek to swim. He pretended to be a frog and he could crouch and jump just like one! He clowned around, and I loved it. He was forever sticking a biscuit in his overalls pocket (saving it for tough times?). One time, our dog Rex dug up a biscuit he had hidden and took the dirty, nasty thing to Paul. When Paul went to Aunt Mattie's, he would ask for a biscuit first thing. Biscuits must not have helped a whole lot though, for he never gained much weight. He was so lovable. Our brother Gee Gee was the main farm hand when Daddy was at work.

Paul was his helper. Paul was as skinny as a fence post and was always hungry. He always carried a biscuit or two in his pants pocket. Sometimes he would share his stash with Rex, our faithful dog. Sometimes Rex would go dig up a biscuit he had buried and bring it to Paul. Guess he knew when Paul's pockets were empty!

Paul was the clown of the family. Seems like everything he did or said ended up being funny. He sure saw the bright side of life. That's a gift from God. Gee Gee was fifteen years old; Paul was thirteen, that summer. Yvonne, the oldest sibling, was nineteen years old and Wilma was next in line. She was seventeen. Yvonne was dating Jerry Stover and they planned to be married soon. Wilma was dating Herbert Turner.

The girls always helped Mother with the cooking and house cleaning. Everyone in those days had lots of work to do. I always thought Mother and Daddy planned things out so well because they had two girls and then two boys and then two more girls with two years between each child, except for six years between Paul and Patty.

Patty, always fighting my battles for me at school. She was my heroine. She was always my best friend. I don't remember us ever having a fight, or even harsh words. She is still my heroine!

Our family had demanding times, more than I can remember. But there was a strong cord of love wrapped around us which has endured the tests of time and we are all still best friends and love each other with a strong enduring kind of love.

We had a lot of troubles, but we had enjoyed a cheerful home.

MUSIC IN OUR FAMILY

Our family really loved music. The children learned lots of songs just listening to Daddy and Mother singing around the house. Mother had an organ, and we love to hear her play it and sing mostly hymns. In my memory I can still hear my beautiful, dark haired, blue-eyed 5-foot 2-inch oldest sister, Yvonne, sitting with Patty and me on that moss covered rock in the path we walked to go to Pax or just to go sit there in the evening and watch the sunset and sing one of our favorites: "Red Sails in The Sunset", a love song Daddy and Mother often sung.

Much of our lives revolved around music. Daddy always was whistling a happy tune or sometimes singing. Now that our younger son, Kevin, is older and now has salt/pepper hair he looks like Daddy and has the same kind of temperament that Daddy had --very patient, soft spoken, never showing anger.

What a heritage we have inherited by having the kind of parents and siblings we had. What a heritage we have - not so much in worldly goods but in character building, work ethic and treating your fellow man with kindness and helpfulness. That is the kind of love Jesus talked about and portrayed. Mother was the glue that held us all together.

Mother and Daddy's way of discipline was to set us down and talk with us about our behavior. Occasionally a pat on our backside spoke louder than words, but that didn't happen too often. The older siblings helped in the general scheme of things. They taught us things they had already experienced.

Throughout the years of my life, I had kept journals; never realizing that they would come in handy when I finally got around to writing the story of my family's and my life. I finally got around to writing about this when I got older. I started writing when I was in my late seventy's; now I am 86 years old! I have books to write and some pictures to paint.

Not that my life has been so spectacular, but everyone has a story to tell and those who feel compelled to tell it will write their book and do the thing you feel led to do, because God has placed a desire in your heart to do something with your life. Someone else may need to read something you write to encourage them on their life journey. So, write that book! Paint those pictures! Sing your songs! Or whatever you feel is your destiny! The things you "dream" about may be a desire our Lord has placed deep down in your innermost being. So, let me urge you to do the thing or things you have thought about so long because that just may be your destiny. Get started! The hardest part of any journey or project is just to get started. Mile by mile, life's a trial; but inch by inch, it's a cinch!" Author Unknown.

When we lived up in "Brunk Holler," we did not have many luxuries most people had even then and especially now. We didn't have electricity or bathrooms and we used kerosene lamps for light. These were glass bottom lamps which contained kerosene oil (something like diesel oil). There was a transparent glass globe that fit into the base. A heavy cloth wick ran from the bottom part to a wick holder in the next part and one would light the wick with a match, if you had some, or make a roll out of the Sears & Roebuck catalog and light it from the stove or fireplace fire. Usually, a family had three to five kerosene lamps to light the rooms of a house.

I would like to think of old timey things and share these with the grandchildren so they will know about the old things and old ways. A passing era of our time here on earth when we as a family used to lay on a quilt out beside the house. I remember those times so well. We would laugh, talk, and sing and anything else that even came to mind. Usually something came up, often in the form of Paul doing something comical! He was so much fun. When he didn't come up with something funny to make us laugh, Patty would come up with something. We could hear the creek farther away, but still close enough to hear it rippling over the rocks.

Daddy and Mother taught us a love of God, family, people, and nature. We all inherited a love of nature. In the fall, when the leaves were dressed out in such brilliant colors; winter was even pretty with all the trees wearing their lovely coats of white. And is there no one in the world who does not love the wonderfully warmer days and much more sunshine of spring? The assorted colors of blossoms on the trees are enough to delight even the hardest heart.

When Wilma used to pull us up and down the frozen creek,

it was a beautiful Winter Wonderland. The trees - the limbs, hung over the creek making an archway for us to skate under (or ride on our cardboard sleds) which Wilma so gladly pulled. Patty and I would hug each other tightly and laugh and yell as over the icy stream we fled. Life was so much fun then! To me, it is a wonderful thing that I can remember so much at such a young age! Were it not for that, I could never write this book!

Daddy took us over to the creek and we played in the water. He knew things about the woods. He took out his pocketknife and cut large pieces of tree bark off a couple of trees and we took our spoons and scraped off the good tasting stuff inside of the bark. I don't know what kind of trees they were, maybe maple or birch. I know sometimes Paul, Gee Gee, Patty, and I would break off a birch limb and chew on the birch bark like it was chewing gum, but we wouldn't swallow it, just chew it, then spit it out.

Daddy was always humming a tune or whistling. He taught us how to sing. I don't know how he knew four-part harmony, but he taught Patty and me to sing parts other than soprano. He taught us how to sing alto and tenor. We could sing surprisingly good as a trio. We sang mostly hymns, but also other popular songs. We could switch parts if another part suited one's voice better. Daddy's favorite song was "Life's Railway to Heaven" which printed in this book. Mother and Daddy's favorite love songs were: "I'll Take You Home Again, Kathleen" and Mother loved "My Wild Irish Rose" and "You Are My Sunshine." Times were hard during the 1930s and 40s. The older siblings taught us important things. And I don't remember our family raising our voices against each other and Mother and Daddy were an inspiration to us - Precious Memories!

Porter Wagoner Lyrics

"Life's Railway to Heaven" Porter Wagoner Lyrics from Amazon Music

Life is like a mountain railroad
With an engineer that's brave
We must make the run successful
From the cradle to the grave
Watch the curves, the hills, the tunnels
Never falter never fail
Keep your hand upon the throttle
And your eye upon the rail.

Blessed Savior Thou wilt guide us
Till we reach that blissful shore
Where the angels wait to join us
In God's praise forevermore

As you roll across the trestle
Spanning Jordan's swelling tide
You behold the Union Depot
Into which your train will glide
There'll you meet the superintendent
God the father, God the son
With the hearty joyous plaudit
Weary pilgrim welcome home

Blessed Savior Thou wilt guide us
Till we reach that blissful shore
Where the angels wait to join us
In God's praise forevermore

"LIFE'S RAILWAY TO HEAVEN"
By Ailene Deck

Life is like a mountain railroad
With an engineer that's brave
We must make the run successful
From the cradle to the grave
Watch the curves, the hills, the tunnels
Never falter, never fail.
Keep your hand upon the throttle
And your eye upon the rail

Blessed Savior, thou wilt guide us
Til we reach that blissful shore
Where the angels wait to join us
In thy praise forever more

Verse 2
You will roll up grades of trial
You will cross the bridge of strife
See that Christ is your conductor
On this lightning train of life

Always <u>mindful</u> of obstruction
Do your duty, <u>never</u> fail
Keep your hand upon the throttle
And your eye upon the rail

You will <u>often</u> find obstruction
Look for <u>storms</u> of wind and rain
On a hill, or curve, or trestle
They will <u>almost</u> ditch your train
Put your <u>trust</u> alone in Jesus
Never falter, <u>never</u> fail
Keep your hand upon the throttle
And your eye upon the rail

As you roll <u>across</u> the trestle
Spanning Jordan's <u>swelling</u> tide
You <u>behold</u> the <u>union</u> depot
Into <u>which</u> your <u>train</u> will glide
There you'll meet the superintendent
God the father, God the son
With the hearty, <u>joyous</u> plaudit
"Weary pilgrim, <u>welcome</u> home"

Another one of Daddy's favorites was the **"Haven of Rest."**

Verse 1
My soul in sad exile was out on life's sea,
so burdened with sin and distressed,
till I heard a sweet voice,

saying make me your choice,
and I entered the haven of rest.

Chorus:

I've anchored my soul,
in the haven of rest.
I'll sail the wild seas no more,
The tempest may beat
O'er the wild, stormy deep;
in Jesus I'm safe evermore.

Verse 2

Oh come to the savior,
He patiently waits,
To save by his power divine,
Come anchor your soul,
In the haven of rest,
and say my beloved is mine.

Written by George D. Moore and H.L. Gilmore

Mother's Favorite Song was, **"In the Garden."**

Verse 1:

I come to the garden alone,
While the dew is still on the roses;
And the Voice I hear falling on my ear,
The son of God discloses.

Chorus:

And He walks with me, and He talks with me;
And He tells me I am his own;
And the joy we share as we tarry there
None other has ever known.

He speaks and the sound of His voice
Is so sweet the birds hush their singing
And the melody that He gave to me
Within my heart is ringing.

Repeat Chorus

Verse 3:

I'd stay in the garden with Him,
Though the night around me be falling,
But He bids me go, through the voice of woe,
His voice to me is calling.

Repeat Chorus

C. Austin Mills, Lyrics and Music

You Are My Sunshine

You are my sunshine, my only sunshine.
You make me happy when skies are gray.
You'll never know dear how much I love you.
Please don't take my sunshine away.

The other night dear as I lay sleeping,
I dreamed I held you in my arms.
But, when I awoke dear, I was mistaken,
Someone else had stolen your charms.

Repeat first verse

Mother used to sing the songs to us and others. But the two I have listed here; I seem to feel that they were her favorites. I know that "In the Garden" was her favorite hymn.

SNOW ICE CREAM – DECEMBER 1939

It was Christmas time - a magical time for a four-year old. My Daddy, brothers, Gee Gee and Paul, sister, Patty and I were all bundled up and ready to do one of our favorite winter chores: looking for that perfect Christmas tree!

Gee Gee and Paul filled the old wooden sleigh with straw, harnessed ol' Dan to it, and gave him a sweet treat - a couple lumps of sugar and were waiting for us to get on board. Dan was chomping at the bit, excited about getting out to run in the snow. The year was 1939. It was only two more days 'til Christmas and excitement was in the air!

Daddy took the reins and we started out. Soon ol' Dan was pulling us up, up, up the hill to the top where the prettiest fir trees grew. The steamy breath of ol' Dan was producing thick, white frosty streams against the frigid winter air. The stubble left over from the autumn corn crop crunched underneath the runners of the sleigh.

"Daddy, don't go so fast." I yelled.

"Hold on baby, we're almost to the top. Let's sing a song on the way up." Someone started "Dashing through the snow in a one-horse open sleigh, O'er the field we go, laughing all the way."

There was snow - lots of it! And ol' Dan was doing his best; the steam of his breath blasting forth from flared nostrils making vapor like a steam locomotive! His sides were heaving with the effort he was willingly putting forth. The singing spurred him on. He knew he was loved, and he returned that love by his faithfulness and demanding work. Daddy coaxed, "Come on, Dan, just a little further and you can rest and have another good treat (an apple probably).

Ol' Dan understood and soon we were at the top, as if fairies had poured grease on the runners to ease his burden and urge him on. As the final words of "Jingle Bells" echoed across the hills and valley; Dan pulled up to the rows of trees, all frosty and beautiful with the snow sparkling like diamonds as the sun sprung up over the range of mountain tops. We all scampered out of the sleigh as ol' Dan began chomping on the apple he found in Daddy's jacket pocket.

We happily ran through the snow-covered field, looking for the prettiest tree and found a beautiful balsam fir, which we all agreed upon as being the best one. It smelled so good! Then Daddy happened to think of our neighbor who lived up over the hill from our farm and couldn't get out to get her a tree. So, Gee Gee and Paul cut down two trees, so we could deliver one to Mrs. Rhodie Davis.

After loading the trees, we headed down the hill toward our

cabin. Smoke curled up from the chimney of our log cabin and the smell of the wood fire drifted up to us. Gee Gee took the reins, and we went flying down the hill! Daddy was laughing heartily, and we all were laughing, but I was hanging on to Paul for dear life! We loved the wind in our faces, but Patty and I were a little frightened that we would turn over! Our descent was rapid, and the return trip seemed quite short.

Stomping the snow off our feet so that Yvonne and Wilma wouldn't yell at us for tracking up their clean kitchen floor, we carried our prize into the living room to show it off to Mother and the girls.

The smell of sugar cookies and gingerbread men wafted from the kitchen from the coal stove where Yvonne and Wilma were doing the Christmas baking. Mother was making her delicious donuts and they made our mouths water. We didn't often get treats like this, but somehow Daddy had saved up enough for the ingredients for the goodies.

"Cocoa's ready," Wilma called. "Come and get it." "But Gee Gee, go stomp that snow off your boots first. We just mopped the kitchen floor!"

We soon got the tree up and began making decorations for it. We placed the popcorn chain, the paper snowflakes, and angels we had been making for some time on the tree.

The beautiful, shiny figures that we had made from chewing gum wrappers were really eye catching. Every time Wilma's boyfriend, Herbert Turner, came to be with Wilma, he always had sticks of gum in his shirt pocket, and I would run and make a jump toward him, knowing he would catch me and give me a stick of gum. The inner wrapping was foil and we saved all of these to make shiny ornaments, when Christmas time rolled around.

The tree was the focal point for Mother to see from her bed in the living room. Daddy had placed a bed near the windows so she could enjoy the beautiful handiwork of God. She would often say that Our Father was the Master Painter, when she looked at a beautiful sunrise, sunset, a rainbow, the birds, the flowers, and the trees. She always appreciated our beautiful world made by Father God. I am still thankful that I got my love of nature from my parents and from Yvonne.

Mother's face was a little less pale today with all the good excitement. Nothing made her happier than to see her family happy. We placed the small nativity set that Paul had whittled from birch wood on the bedside table.

Mother summoned her strength and went to the old pump organ Grandpa Pittman (her father) had given her and began to play Christmas carols. Our voices rang out in praise to the Christ Child, who had come to set us all free from our sins and destruction, if we would accept His gift of Salvation. In my mind's eye, I can see it all now, indelibly stamped on my memory, along with other precious memories of our humble home and family. Little did we know that it would be our last Christmas to spend together, ever again.

Mother had her own recipe for snow ice cream. In those days (1939) there were lots of families who didn't have a refrigerator or even an ice box. We had neither, but ingenuity provided many alternatives for the necessities of life.

SNOW ICE CREAM
Recipe by Lelia Pittman Brunk

In a clean large kettle or dishpan, scoop up clean snow after you have removed the top of the mound of snow, so that you know it's clean. (You know that dogs, cats, and other animals urinate in the snow!)

Ingredients:

- Snow and Sugar (at least three cups).
- One can evaporated milk - if you are lucky enough to have it! - or Whipping cream.
- Vanilla flavoring - the all-natural kind, if possible, rather than the imitation kind.
- Optional: Any other kind of flavoring, if you have it, for variety. Almond flavoring blends well with vanilla.

Method:

Slowly and carefully add cream to the snow, stirring gently.

- Add sugar. Start with 2 cups but add more if needed.
- Add flavoring (1 Tablespoon).
- Never stir vigorously, always gently.
- Keep the right consistency by adding more snow and

maybe more sugar. Work quickly.

- Pour ice cream into shallow pan, cover and set it outside in the snow. Cover it with the snow. Temperature must be cold so, choose your best day. Allow it to freeze. Then bring inside, dish it up, and enjoy!

ELDERBERRY WINE 1939

We had a good garden that year in 1939 from which we harvested good vegetables. We were always glad when the green beans "came in". Sometimes we cooked them with small "new" potatoes in them. And we always had green onions out of the garden in the summertime. Sometimes we mixed lettuce and onions together to make a salad and made dressing out of vinegar, sugar, salt, pepper, and hot bacon grease.

Summer food was so good. We often had good fresh tomatoes, raw carrots, radishes, celery, and cooked beets. Sometimes we had cooked greens - turnip greens, mustard greens, and creasy greens (creasy greens are like watercress) that we just found growing wild - not planted. They came up from last year's crop and so we called them, "volunteers." Daddy liked them with vinegar poured on them, but Patty and I did not like them.

Everyone was happiest when the corn was ready. Patty and I could go to the garden and pick enough ears of corn for the whole family and shuck them, too. After the ears boiled, we smothered them with butter and salted them. It was mouthwatering! In the wintertime, we ate canned food and had lots of brown (pinto) beans cooked with meat seasoning, salt, pepper, and water to make them "soupy." They cooked all day in a big pot on the back part of the stove; slow cooking made them extremely tasty. We always had fried potatoes cooked with onions and delicious corn bread with butter. That was one of our favorite meals. We usually had pickles, cucumbers, tomatoes, squash, and raw onions on the table when we cooked brown beans in the summer. Beans were a good protein food our older sisters told us.

They stayed busy all that summer canning the food. They would can around eight hundred quart-size jars. We would dig up the potatoes, sweet potatoes, turnips, and any other vegetables that grew underground and put them in the cellar. We would eat his food during the winter months, along with apples, walnuts, and anything else that could be kept several months in a cool cellar.

All the kids went out into the woods to pick black berries. Boy, we loved to eat them while picking them! The best ones grew in the hardest places to get to with briers and brush to get through. The days were hot and oppressive, and we all got sweaty and tired, but eating our fill of berries saved the day.

Sometimes we would run into a snake. Most of the time it scared us girls (little and big girls) half to death, but Paul and Gee Gee laughed at us and called us scaredy cats and sometimes chased us around with that ugly snake hanging on the end of a hoe or other farm implement - or a big stick if nothing else was handy.

Then we would have to clean the berries, each one individually and wash them. Then at suppertime we would enjoy blackberry cobbler. Such a treat! Daddy liked milk on his. We would also pick raspberries, blueberries, and grapes. Yvonne and Wilma would make jelly out of them and can it. One rarely hears about elderberries these days. They were used for making elderberry jelly and elderberry wine. They grow wild, mostly near a creek or lake.

One summer, I remember finding a big crock sitting behind the kitchen stove. A crock is a big, heavy piece of pottery usually used for churning milk to make buttermilk and butter. Inside, grape juice, turned out to be Paul and Gee Gee.'s elderberry wine. All I knew about wine was that one used fruit, mashed it, poured water into it, covered it, and left it in a warm place to ferment. I don't know how that juice was processed or how many days it took to ferment, but I did know one had to put quite a bit of sugar in it. To this day, in my mind, there is a mystery surrounding this subject. I have often wondered if Mother knew about it and if so, why didn't she or Daddy make the boys get rid of the forbidden alcoholic substance?

In the summer, all the kids had jobs to do, but there was leisure time for playing and visiting friends, swimming in the creek, and reading. I was two or three years old when we moved from Brooklyn to the log house up in the hollow. I went to Brooklyn, West Virginia once after our marriage and saw the little run-down house in which I had been born and lived a couple of years.

PAUL AND THE RACCOON

PAUL SYDNEY
BRUNK

"Mommy! Mommy! Hurry Paul's bleeding, dying," I screamed on that sweltering summer day. Patty was running into the house to get Mother. Soon, they both came running out of the house. I was standing there in shock, while blood spurted out of Paul's head. The blood had already made a dark puddle beside the wire and wooden cage he was making for the raccoon he had caught. He still held the hatchet in his right hand, had crumbled to his knees on the ground and was as pale as a ghost. He looked as if all the blood had drained from his face and left it blank, like a sheet of paper never written upon.

Mother ran to his crumpled and lifeless-looking body, lifted my thirteen-year-old skinny brother, held him to her breast as she checked his wrist and then his neck to find a pulse.

"Patty, hurry and get an armful of towels. Dip one in the bucket of water. We must get him to the doctor, quickly! Hurry! Patty took off, and I took the hatchet out of his tightly clutched hand and threw it, hard, as if it were an evil thing!

Patty was back in a flash. Mother took a thick white towel and held it tightly to the big slash in his skull. We all started down the lane as quickly as Mother could walk, carrying her precious burden.

I could not quit crying, and tears were rolling down Patty's pretty face. She kept poking me and whispering, "Be quiet! You are upsetting Mother!" So, I shushed up. Paul had never moved. We wondered, "Is he dead?" Patty whispered, "he probably fainted, because of losing his blood. He might be all right."

Mother did not talk at all. It was all she could do to carry Paul. I am sure she didn't have breath enough to talk, also.

We had already crossed the creek, gone up the little hill and were halfway down the path that led to the ball field near Weirwood. Thank God it was cool here on the path with all the trees of the forest giving us shade. It was at least a mile to Dr. Alfred Hunter's office in Pax. I wondered if Paul could make it 'til we got there. I had never been so scared in my life!

Soon, Paul started groaning and we all felt relieved. At least, we knew he was still alive. The towel on his head was all bloody. Mother stopped and sat down in the middle of the path, cradling Paul like a baby. Patty handed Mother another towel. Mother said, "hand me the wet one; maybe the coolness will help." She held the cold cloth on the wound and kept her hand on it, pressing down. That seemed to help. The bleeding slowed down.

Paul began to rouse up a little, tried to sit up, with Mother supporting him. Another minute or two and he stood up, shakily at first. Patty and I stood beside him to help hold him up if necessary. He said, "I can walk." Mother arose and put her arms around him, and we started out again. "Thank you, God," I'm sure we were all thinking.

We crossed the ball field and came to the railroad tracks. The sun was beating down so hard, the sweat was pouring off all of us, especially Paul and Mother. Mother had been feeling unwell for quite some time, and we were worried about her. I know Patty was praying with all her might and so was I. "Dear God, please help us make it to Dr. Alfred's, I prayed inwardly. Please give Paul and Mommy the strength to make it."

Long waves of heat rose from the tracks like long magic fingers tickling the afternoon air. It just looked hot as we looked farther down the tracks. We had, I guess, at least another half mile to walk and the hot sun was unmerciful as we trudged along. Paul was stumbling but was putting up a brave front to try to prove he could do it. I admired his courage. Mother had to change towels once again. Good thing Patty had brought about five.

Now the post office was in sight and town hall and Givens

tavern and both Canterbury's stores. We would soon be there. "Sure hope Dr. Alfred is in," Patty said. It was about one o'clock in the afternoon.

We walked into the outer office. There were only two other people there. I can't, for the life of me, remember who they were, although I'm pretty sure I knew them.

Dr. Alfred came out of his office. One look, and he exclaimed, "What in the world happened here?" Patty tearfully explained,

"Paul was building a cage for his raccoon and raised his hatchet up too far, hit his head and slashed his head open. He's been bleeding all the way here. We thought he would die before we got here!"

Dr. Alfred picked him up, carried him to his exam table and gently laid him down and began to work on him. Mother stayed in there with him but made us go into the outer room. It was a stone building, and we were thankful that it was so cool. We sat down and tried to pull ourselves together. We were both shaking, and a lady and gentleman came over, put their arms around us and spoke comforting words to us. It sure helped to calm us down.

The man walked over to Ed Canterbury's store and bought a grape soda for us; we always called it "pop." Boy, was it good! That helped a whole lot! I've often thought back and remembered their kindness. Jesus said, "that He blesses people who give a thirsty person a cup of cold water in His name. I'm sure that couple got a real blessing out of giving us that much-needed bottle of "pop".

Dr. Alfred got the bleeding stopped, shaved off part of Paul's hair, stitched up the wound, gave him some shots and some medicine for pain and we were through.

You know, to this day, I don't know how we got back home. I don't remember walking back and I'm sure we didn't. Paul wasn't able to walk back. Neither was Mother. I don't know if someone drove us home or what. But somehow, we got back there.

Gee Gee finished the raccoon pen and took care of the animal for a while and then turned it loose, back out into the wild. I never did know where everyone else was that day. I guess Daddy was at work. It was summer, so no one was in school. I guess I'll never know. But the important thing was we made it through a terrifying experience, and I learned a lesson in courage from Paul, Mother and Patty and learned to appreciate the kindness of strangers and, the goodness of God in answering our prayers and giving us the strength to keep going, under trying circumstances.

We learned lots of hard lessons growing up during challenging times. And if sometimes, we couldn't see the lesson, life was trying to teach us, we had wise parents and caring sisters and brothers to teach us and help us learn.

I have always been thankful for and appreciative of those

people in my life who contributed to helping me become the person I am today. No one crosses our path accidentally. God orchestrates it all, I believe.

DEPRESSION DAYS

Our Log Cabin Home in Brunk Hollow

LOG CABIN IN

BRUNK HOLLOW

In the early 1920's Daddy and Mother lived up in the northern part of the state of West Virginia at Clarksburg and in Fairmont. Wilma, Gee Gee, and Paul were born there. Daddy was a salesman for General Electric.

My sisters told me about the nice houses up north. One was a big, two-story house by the river at the Clarksburg location. I know it must have been terribly hard to leave a nice house like that and move into a coal company house and then two or three years later move to a cabin in the "Holler". But the Great Depression which began in 1929 had knocked the props out from under many families. Lots of folks lost their homes during those tough times. People had to be resourceful and work a lot harder and longer to feed their families.

There were very few places where a man could find a job. The southern region of West Virginia was famous for its coal producing mines. The coal in this area was good coal for making steel. So, Daddy and Mother moved the family to southern West Virginia where Daddy found work. We moved to a small town named Brooklyn in Fayette County, down in the New River Gorge (which is now famous because it is a national river and has the world's second highest, single span bridge, crossing the gorge.) The river has brought in lots of tourist trade now because people from all over the world come here to go whitewater rafting, parachuting from the bridge, and rock repelling. Back then, though, there was just coal in these mountains to mined and sent out and sold to the nations of the world.

We built our cabin on land that was owned by Aunt Hattie, another one of Daddy's sisters. She owned property on our side of the mountain and a lot of land on the other side of the mountain where she had a nice big house. She told Daddy we could live there on her land as long as it was necessary.

Daddy, Uncle Guy, Gee Gee, Paul and two cousins, Alfred Tyree and Kenneth Cole built a log cabin, which became our home in the hollow at Knob Branch and later became known as Brunk Hollow. About a mile to the north was the town of Pax (meaning "peace") where we went to school, did grocery shopping, got our mail, and went to Dr. Alfred Hunter when the need arose. About a mile from Weirwood to Pax, going south, we could either walk on the railroad track or on the curvy hard top road, which ran parallel to Paint Creek.

After crossing the ball field, we would walk up the little path through the woods to our house. The dirt road upon which Daddy traveled in his model T ran parallel to the little path. The trees hung out over the road making it look like an archway or a beautiful tunnel. I thought it looked like a forest and it smelled "woodsy." The mountain laurels and ivy were all over the place. The woods looked like a postcard at every change of the seasons. I used to argue with myself as to which of the seasons was the prettiest. Mother and Daddy loved God's beautiful handiwork and I think that is why I'm so overwhelmed by the world's beauty all *around me.*

Brooklyn was a coal mining camp. The owners of the mines had built the houses for their workers and families. The houses all looked alike. Most were four room houses, no indoor plumbing, but I think we had electricity. The company took out the rent money before the men received their pay.

The coal company owned a company store. Most coal miners shopped there because many didn't have a car with which to go shopping elsewhere. So, the miners would have the items charged to their account. The prices were higher at their store.

At the end of the pay period, most of the miners had used up all the money they had made to pay the house rent and the company store. If they had any money coming to them, they were happy on payday. But if they had used up all the money they had made, the accountant would draw a curvy line through their pay stub and the miners would say, "All I got this pay period was a "snake."

I guess Daddy drew a "snake" many times. Tennessee Ernie Ford had a song out about mining, which included the phrase "I owe my soul to the company store." It was about coal miners, back breaking work, poor working conditions and always being in debt to the company store.

In many coal mines the roof top was so low the workers could never stand. If the roof top was three feet high, it would be like working bent over under your kitchen table digging out the "black gold" with a pick and shovel. The darkness in there was over-whelming. It was always damp; lots of times they worked in standing and dank water. Their only light was a small carbide lantern hooked onto the front of their hard hat. Sometimes the roof was so low, they had to lie on their bellies to work. Some mines were labeled as "hot" meaning the deadly methane gas would build up to a high degree and could kill all the workers. In the early days, they kept a canary in a cage in each section where men were working. If the canary started dying, the men knew that they must get out of there quickly.

It was a well-known fact that my Dad could load coal quicker than the others. Each man had a cart. When it was filled with coal, he marked it with his number tag and started on another cart to load. No wonder Daddy was exhausted when he came home. These days everything has become so mechanized, and computers do much of the work. But coal mining is still dangerous work.

In the early days of coal mining before my Dad's time, they used mules to pull the cars full of coal to the front of the mines. The poor mules had adapted to the darkness inside, but most of the time they went blind. So far as I know, they lived in the mine and if they were ever brought outside, they couldn't endure the bright daylight. Later, they laid tracks in the mines and had motorized engines to pull the coal cars around.

One thing that everyone feared was a cave-in called a slate fall. Sometimes if the top hadn't been "shored" up well with big timbers, the top would give way and fall. Many miners were killed or injured this way.

Times were hard. But I guess I was shielded from knowing that. And there was talk of a war in Europe. We were Depression-era children, but didn't know it, because in our house, I just remembered the good times. I remember the love which flowed from one family member to the next. I don't remember hearing harsh words, angry voices or squabbles among the children. And over it all was mother and father who loved each other deeply and loved their children. They taught love by their example. I consider myself very blessed to have been born into such a family where peace and love prevailed.

A WONDERFUL CHRISTMAS- 1939

Togetherness is a family necessity sadly lacking in our society these days in the twenty-first century. If we could have more "family togetherness," we would see a dramatic decline in crime and violence in our world today.

The kerosene lamps burned lower as Daddy read the Christmas story from Luke, chapter two. I've always loved that story. And it's true! Then bedtime! Up the steps to the big common bedroom where we all slept, Patty and I in our corner, Gee Gee and Paul in their corner, Yvonne and Wilma in their corner and Mother and Daddy now in the bed downstairs.

Several times during the night, I could hear Daddy putting more wood in the stove. The chimney, which came up through the upstairs area, made it warm in our attic bedroom. Yvonne and Wilma's bed sat nearest to the heat. And sometimes, on the coldest nights, Patty and I would slip over and crawl in bed with them to get toasty warm. They never complained and were happy to oblige.

The next morning, we knew that Santa had come that night with a few home¬made gifts everyone had made over the past few weeks. Chiffon hankies and a scarf for Mother made from an old worn-out dress, from Yvonne and Wilma--Patty and I helped hem them. Everyone had pooled nickels, dimes, and quarters together to get Daddy a new, much needed dinner bucket to take to the coal mines.

Miraculously, despite her illness, Mother had made a skirt and blouse each for Wilma and Yvonne and dolls for Patty and me. Daddy had made a new snow sled for Gee Gee and Paul. He also had bought Christmas goodies for the whole family - ribbon candy, peppermint candy canes, gumdrops, lollipops, a box of chocolate covered cherries and some fruits and nuts. We had a wonderful Christmas and a delicious Christmas dinner.

In the afternoon, we played some games. We had a checkerboard and checkers and we liked to make up stories with everyone adding their bit to it, no matter how ridiculous it sounded.

The sunset cast a beautiful pink, purple and bluish glow on the western horizon. Soon, a banana moon peeped through the trees and the moon light, shining on the snow-covered yard, made it look like millions of diamonds had fallen out of the sky.

We all went to bed with full tummies, feeling rich and happy. What a wonderful Merry Christmas we had enjoyed!

MOONLIGHT AND ROSES
JUNE 10, 1940

MATTIE, LOTTIE AND LILLIAN
WITH WILMA AND YVONNE

Moonlight flooded the front yard and cast a jewel-like radiance upon the pink rambling roses that crept across the front of the smoke house and the beautiful red ones that grew beside the cabin door. The beautiful hollyhocks and gladiolas that grew along the front and side of the house added to the loveliness of the evening. The evening air was full of the fragrance of the flowers Mother loved so well. The sound of a whip-or-will added to the beauty and loveliness of the occasion.

We were having a tea party to celebrate Mother's birthday and Patty and I had been busy setting up our little play table with our little China tea set which had beautiful hummingbirds painted on the tea pot and cups. This was such a special occasion! Mother was going to be 38-years old tomorrow, June 10,1940.

We had found a lace curtain which served very well as an elegant tablecloth. We didn't have a beautiful vase for the flowers, but we wrapped a piece of pretty material around a canning jar and put roses in it for the centerpiece.

So, everything was ready. We had made the tea and found some cookies in the kitchen. We led mother outside with her eyes closed. "Now you can open your eyes," said six-year-old Patty.

"Oh, how lovely, Mother said. "You ladies have outdone yourself." We were pretending that we were grown-up ladies who had invited her over for a birthday party. She played right along with us as we talked grown-up lady talk. Mother might wear faded dresses and have old worn-out furniture and live in a small cabin in a West Virginia hollow, but she was born for elegance. She had a way of making you feel that way. It was the twinkle in her pretty brown eyes or the quiet way she went through life with its hardships and didn't complain or hardly notice she was poor. Everyone who knew her loved her. There was just something about her that attracted people to her.

Mother could barely fit her tall frame into our kid-sized chairs which Daddy had made along with the table, but she sat there as straight and dignified as a queen.

Patty was pouring the tea, since I was only four years old at the time and would turn five when October rolled around. Patty would soon be seven later in June.

"Mmmmm, best tea I ever tasted," Mother said smiling. "And these cookies are wonderful. You two must have worked hard all evening preparing this nice birthday celebration." Patty and I, of course, were just beaming.

If Daddy's car had been there, we could have had music and dancing, but Daddy was still at work. We had no electricity, but sometimes on a Saturday, Mother or one of the older girls made candy or popcorn and cocoa. We played games like checkers or Tiddly Winks. Mother and Daddy always knew how to help the children have fun. When we had lived in Brooklyn, Daddy built the only gym set that was in the work camp. All the neighboring children came and had a good time on the "slicky slide," the swings, the monkey bars and the sand box. You didn't have to be rich to have a good time, just as long as you had parents who could act like kids once in a while.

Sometimes on a night when Daddy wasn't working, like a Saturday night, he would park the car beside the open window and hook up the big, tall radio to the car battery and we could have music.

So, as we would often do -- we three just sang some songs. "Beautiful Dreamer" was one of our favorites and Mother had a favorite hymn called "In the Garden" and, of course, "You Are My Sunshine." Any time Mother sang that song, she would give us a hug. We knew we were her sunshine, and she was certainly our sunshine.

Sometimes on those Saturday nights, when we had music and the family was all together, Mother and Daddy would dance. We just loved to watch them dance. It was so pretty to see them holding each other close and swaying to the music. Mother would make a batch of candy and it was party time!

The moon climbed higher in the sky and crafted a beautiful picture as it peeped between the branches of the tall trees surrounding our yard. The creek, on the back side of the cabin, just beyond the garden patch, made a soft gurgling sound. The dew began to fall. And our party ended.

As we put away the tea service in the old worn-out cabinet, we heard the unmistakable sound of Daddy's Ford Model T chugging up the road. Even when we were in bed, or off picking blackberries or doing the things kids do at play; we knew how far up the road he had come, by the sound of the shifting gears as he slowed down for the ruts and chug - holes and then the idling motor, down by the creek as he got out to open the big gate and cross the shallow creek.

It was our bedtime, but Mother let us linger just a little longer until Daddy got to the house and gave us a big hug before we took off up the stairs to the little bedroom under the eaves.

You could have known when he was coming, even if you could not hear the old Model T coming. Mother's eyes always got that glow when she knew he was coming.

How did she do it? Six kids, nothing to work with, a little log house, no electricity, no nice clothes to wear and she was only thirty -eight years old! Looking back, I guess it was just because she loved Daddy and us kids.

We heard him come in, whistling as usual. We knew he was bone - tired; miners always were. Mother had his bath water heating on the stove, ready to pour into the galvanized wash tub sitting in the middle of the kitchen floor; the oven door opens to give out heat, a quilt hung over the open doorway between the kitchen and living room. There was corn bread in the iron skillet, a pot of brown beans simmering on the stove, fried potatoes, and fresh garden onions all waiting for Daddy to eat after his bath.

As he ate and they quietly talked, Patty and I lay in our bed upstairs and watched the moonlight cast shadows on the walls and floor, as it shone through the big oak tree that stood outside our window. Yvonne and Wilma were out with their boyfriends, Yvonne with Jerry, and Wilma with Herbert, and would soon be home.

Suddenly, we heard a loud, piercing sound coming from the

woods! Thump! Four bare feet hit the wood floor at once and down the stairs they flew into the kitchen, where we became tangled up in the quilt hanging on one side of the kitchen door. We aimed for Daddy and jumped on his lap, threw arms around his neck, nearly knocking the breath out of him.

"A bear's out there, Daddy! We heard him! It sounded awful!" I shouted at him.

I thought he'd jump up and grab his gun and take off for the woods! But he just sat there and laughed. I felt just a trifle annoyed! "Did you forget? The boys are camping out tonight. Those weird noises are coming from their cave, and they think they have us all fooled. Now, you two get back to bed and tomorrow when they come in, tell them you saw this huge animal out in the woods and it was headed straight for their cave, and they better be careful or it might come right up to their camp, one of these nights and they won't be able to do a thing, because it's so big and terrible!"

This sounded like such a clever idea that we bounded up those stairs, hopped into bed and for some time we added a lot more to the tale he had started. We would have a delightful story to give Paul and Gee Gee tomorrow!

OUR DEAR MOTHER'S FAILING HEALTH

We had known for a long time that our dear Mother was sick; but we had never thought she wouldn't get well. We knew about the tiredness. She used to move so quickly as she went about her work. During the summer of 1940, she stopped and rested more frequently, sometimes lying down for quite a while. My older sisters Yvonne and Wilma were doing more of the housework, the gardening and summer canning.

Then, there were the trips to the hospital. Daddy took her to the hospital in Beckley several times during that summer. She had been so happy to be able to attend Wilma and Yvonne's graduation from Pax High School in May 1940. She had made the girls' new dresses. They looked so pretty! I don't know where they had gotten their new high-heeled shoes, but I guess Wilma's job at a drug store at Mt. Hope had helped. Yvonne had been doing some house cleaning for Mrs. Akers, one of the high school teachers. Herbert Turner, Wilma's boyfriend, and Jerry Stover, Yvonne's boyfriend, were graduating too. (The reason Yvonne and Wilma graduated at the same time was because Mother and Daddy had held Yvonne back until Wilma could attend school.)

Mother had looked so beautiful in the navy-blue dress she

made for herself. It had a lovely white lace collar. She wore a white hat, shoes and gloves and a string of pearls. Daddy was as handsome as she was pretty! They rarely dressed up like that! Daddy had on a nice, navy-blue suit with all the trimmings. He had a beautiful head of black, slightly curly hair, pretty, blue eyes and light olive-colored skin, as did Mother. Daddy was 5-feet 10-inches tall, and Mother was about 5-feet 6-inches. Neither was overweight. Mother wore a single white rose on her shoulder. Her mother, Grandma Pittman, had died two years before this event. Mother had a challenging time accepting Grandmother's death, my sisters had told me. She always called her mother "Momma." In those days, around Mother's Day in May, every lady wore a red flower to a graduation if her mother was living, and a white one if her mother was deceased.

During that summer of 1940, after graduation, Mother's health steadily got worse. One day, I went around the side of the house, nearest to the creek, to pick a bouquet of flowers for Mommy and there was Daddy, standing alone, leaning against the house, and crying. I rarely saw Daddy cry. He wouldn't tell me what was wrong. He just wiped his eyes, picked me up and in answer to my question, he said, "Oh, just problems, Honey."

But as summer turned into fall, Mother steadily grew worse and finally she stayed in the bed. Daddy moved their bed from the upstairs, down to the living room where she could be near the family, and we could keep her company. She could look out the windows to see God's beautiful handiwork in our lovely wilderness.

Sometime during that summer, or it was autumn; Daddy, Herbert and Wilma took Mother to Johns Hopkins Hospital in Baltimore. Daddy had a newer car, a Plymouth, I believe. Mother was extremely exhausted when they returned. They had run some tests and given her radium treatments. I never knew until years later that she had uterine cancer.

Then before winter set in, Grandpa Pittman had Daddy bring Mother to his house in Beckley so she could be close to the hospital. Wilma and Yvonne took turns staying a week at a time at Grandpa's to take care of her, along with Mother's sister, Aunt Mattie, who lived there also with her family.

When it was Yvonne's turn to go to Grandpa's, Wilma took care of us and things at home. Then Wilma would go the next week and Yvonne took care of us. Yvonne was nineteen and Wilma was seventeen.

After Mother's death, Aunt Mattie asked Daddy if he would let them adopt Patty. But Daddy and Mother always had their minds made up that the children would never be separated so, he wouldn't agree. Since we were in pairs, the two oldest girls were close, Paul and Gee Gee were best buddies and Patty, and I were always like two peas in a pod. It would have been great for Patty to have had Betty for a sister and to live in our grandfather's beautiful home. But as I think of it now, I cannot imagine growing up without her! We were so remarkably close. Always have been! Always will be! I always called her "my sunshine," just like the song Mother use to sing to us, titled, "You are My Sunshine."

MOTHER'S PASSING
DECEMBER 13, 1940

Christmas, 1940, would soon be here. I can't remember if there were any preparations being made to celebrate. Everyone's mind was somewhere else. Mother was at Grandpa Pittman's house in Beckley. She was sick. Nobody told me this, but somehow, I knew. I can remember Daddy taking us there several times. Sometimes the medicine they gave her made her too drowsy to stay awake long.

It is strange that I can't remember very much about our visits to see her. Sometimes I don't know if I dreamed things about her last days or if they really were true. Looking back, I can realize that a five-year-old might not remember such tragic incidents in her life. I had only turned five on October, twenty-eighth that year. Patty had turned seven on June twenty-third. Mother had turned thirty-eight on June tenth.

Some things I recall were the quietness in her room. It was a pretty room, located in the southwest corner at the front of Grandfather's house, just off the end of the wrap-around porch, with its swings and rocking chairs. The room had seven tall windows with pretty, lacy curtains. Grandpa's old clock was ticking so loudly. The picture on the wall at the head of her bed was so pretty. Mother loved beautiful things. The picture was a lovely pastoral picture with children playing near a creek.

Mother lay there so quietly, so beautiful. Her hair was so dark and shiny. I was thinking "how much her hair looks like a pretty bird's wings, iridescent as the sun shone upon it."

She finally aroused and realized we were there. She smiled and said in a soft voice, "I'm so glad to see you all! I love all of you more than you could ever know. My love for you is not dying. It will always go on living. I've been praying for all of you with every heartbeat, and I know God is hearing my prayers. My prayers will be with you as long as you live. After I'm gone, always remember that my prayers will continue for you until we see each other again in our Heavenly Father's House."

She rested a little and we all were trying hard not to let her see our tears. Paul and Gee Gee were working hard trying not to cry. All the girls had tears on our faces. Daddy was going from one to another of us, resting an arm around the boys, stroking our hair, wiping away our tears, as well as his own.

Mother wanted us to remember the important things. She said "keep loving each other. Let nothing separate you to keep you from loving each other, ever. Keep your faith in God and Jesus and remember to pray and read the Bible and go to church. Live the way we've taught you. Keep a dream in your heart and God will help you live your dreams."

Yvonne, Wilma, Gee Gee and Paul gave her a big hug and kissed her on her cheek or forehead. Good, gentle, long hugs, all the time making sure not to hurt her delicate body. And trying not to let her see their tears. Patty and I climbed up on the bed with her and lay there with our arms around her. Daddy came and sat on the side of the bed and held Mommy's hand.

Paul waved good-bye. It was such a sad gesture!

As Patty and I got up to go we said, "I love you, Mommy." She weakly hugged us and said, "Don't ever forget- I'll love you forever." Daddy, Patty, and I left the room. I wasn't thinking about not seeing her anymore. I thought we would come back and see her again. But that did not happen.

How do you handle a thought that you won't ever see your mother again? But later, I began to remember her words that "she would always be with us." That brought some comfort to our empty arms and long days that left us feeling empty. Our sunshine wasn't physically with us, but we knew that God had already made it possible for us to meet again and we'll never again have to say good-bye.

"OUR SUNSHINE IS GONE"

MRS. S. D. BRUNK TAKEN BY DEATH

Funeral Services For Pax Woman Planned Sunday

PAX, Dec. 13.—Mrs. Lillian Pittman Brunk, 38 years old, of Pax, died at the home of her parents, Mr. and Mrs. George Pittman, at Sprague early this morning, following an illness of 15 months. Her death was attributed to cancer.

Born at Central on June 10, 1902, she was the wife of S. D. Brunk, of Pax. She was a member of the Baptist church.

Surviving besides her parents James Gilhooley, Mrs. E. J. Ag-

and husband are six children, Yvonne, Wilma, Patty, Ailene, George, and Paul, all at home; three brothers, Harvey Pittman, and Lonald Pittman, of Sprague; and Jack Pittman, of Beckley; and six sisters, Mrs. Lottie Teel, Mrs. Mattie Bostic, Mrs. Ruth Worley, and Miss Dorothy Pittman, all of Sprague; Mrs. Macel Brunk and Mrs. Lottie Cole, of Beckley.

Funeral services will be conducted at the home of her father, George Pittman, at Sprague Sunday at 2:30 p. m. The Rev. T. E. Pennington, of the Church of the Nazarene in Beckley, will officiate.

Burial will be made in Sunset Memorial Park.

NON-SUPPORT CHARGED

LEWISBURG, Dec. 12—Henry Permenter of near Rainelle was in the Greenbrier county jail Thursday following a hearing in

Our double first cousin, Joy Deason who had stayed with Patty and me while the funeral procession moved on down the hillside road, tried to get our minds off the things that had transpired over the past few hours. But the scenes were already cemented into our minds (and deep into our consciousness). That black hearse was taking our dear MOTHER away!

Patty and I had sat one on either side of Daddy in the big dining room during the service. I don't remember crying. Maybe I did. I guess I did because when I looked at my dear cousins' faces,

I only saw blurred images of Betty, Faye, Sissy, and the others. The service seemed long, but I couldn't tell you a thing that was said or sung.

I am sure there was music because we were a musical family. The big old pump organ was still in the big parlor where all the flowers and the casket were placed. The casket stood in front of the big stained-glass windows. The stained glass was only on the top of the windows and there were five windows, I think. I was always fascinated by those windows. The flowers were all so beautiful. Purple irises, mother's favorite, were in abundance. There were lovely pink gladiolas, another of mother's favorites, and lots of others which I can't name.

But one thing I truly remember were the roses on top of the gray casket. I dearly love roses. There were pink, red, white, and yellow roses, so beautiful. The air was full of the aroma of flowers. Patty and I were holding tightly to Daddy whose face became flooded with tears. I remember looking at Grandpa whose tears rolled silently down his face, and I thought, "I don't think I have ever seen Grandfather cry until now."

I recall the minister from the Nazarene Church standing in front of the crowd quietly speaking words of comfort from the Bible which he held in his hands. At times, my attention traveled to my beautiful new white shoes and pink lacy socks. I had on a real pretty, pink dress and a pink ribbon in my curly, blonde hair. I'll never know who bought Patty's and my outfits that day, but I kind of thought it was either Uncle Guy or Uncle Roy. Patty had on a pretty-green dress, socks, and ribbon in her light brown hair.

Then I wondered if a man could pick out pretty clothes like that or did one of our aunts or cousins help them? I didn't think Daddy ever bought things like this before. Oh well, they were nice to have, and I felt like a princess sitting there. Patty kept crying and I would reach across Daddy's lap to hold her hand and as always, we held hands so tightly. I knew there was love and safety in her hands. She was seven and a half-year old and I was only five. To tell the truth, I can't remember a thing that took place between sitting there and standing upstairs looking out that rain-drenched window.

MY DEAR TEDDY BEAR BROTHER

GEORGE GRIFFITH BRUNK

The night was chilly, but our log cabin was cozy and warm. The kerosene oil lamp burned brightly, as I let out another croupy cough. I was five-years old, and our darling, beautiful thirty-eight-year-old Mother had died of cancer on one of the worst days of my life, December 13,1940. It had only been four weeks since that great tragedy and our family of six children and Daddy were still trying to learn how to cope with such a great loss.

It was the middle of the night and Daddy was fixing a remedy for the croup I so often contracted. I've never learned whether my remembrance of the concoction they gave for croup is correct or not, but I've always thought it was a tablespoon of sugar with a few drops of kerosene oil which somehow loosened the phlegm which was choking me.

Daddy gave me the medicine and I was ready to get back into bed. I am sure Daddy was eager to get back to bed, also. He smiled at me and said, "back up to bed you go and maybe we won't have to get up any more tonight to do this again."

"But Daddy, I don't want to go back to my bed now." I was standing there bare¬footed and in my nightgown. The kerosene lamp was burning lower, and the big old warm morning stove was hot since Daddy had added more wood. The wood made a cheerful, popping, and crackling sound reminding me of popcorn we often enjoyed on frosty winter evenings.

"Well, just where would you like to go, little lady, if not back to your bed?" he asked. "I want to get in bed with Gee Gee." "Why" Daddy asked. "Because it's just like getting into bed with a heating stove," I said.

JOHN GRIFFITH BRUNK

My fifteen-year-old brother, Gee Gee's real name was George Griffith Brunk. His name came from both grandfathers, Mother's father, George Pittman and Daddy's father, John Griffith Brunk. All my growing up years, the family called him Gee Gee. That's the only name I've ever known him by.

I said "Gee Gee's like a big ole teddy bear and he's so warm! I know I'll get better if I sleep the rest of the night with him."

So, I went to his bed, tapped him on the head. He wasn't angry with me for waking him up. He pulled back the covers, smiling that lovable smile of his and I climbed into bed. He wrapped his warm loving arms around me, and I felt snug, safe, and warm, enveloped in a cocoon of Love.

A few years ago, I had surgery. For a get-well gift, Gee Gee, Wilma, Patty, and Yvonne bought me a beautiful white, soft teddy bear with a plaid blue and pink ribbon around its neck. That bear sits on my bed all the time and when I'm feeling blue or lonely, I grab that bear and hug it to me and think of my loving family and how much we have always loved each other. They are all so dear to my heart. And anytime I make a call from West Virginia to California, when Gee Gee would answer the phone, I would say "Hi, my teddy bear brother," and I'd always hear his little chuckle from the other end.

Gee Gee went to Jesus on April 14, 2015, at 3:23 AM in California, but he is still my teddy bear brother.

TRYING TO MAKE IT ON OUR OWN 1941

It was one of those perfect days in May. The year was 1941. Warm rays of sunlight filtered through the soft, green leaves of the big old oak tree which always stood like a sentinel on the hillside over-looking the lovely, quiet spring. Mother always said this was the sweetest, best water she had ever tasted and everyone who drank it agreed.

We lay on our tummies, Patty, and I, and filled ourselves with the sweet cool, clear water. While lying there, we noticed a decent size crawdad (crayfish) on the bottom that decided to be quiet this time. Sometimes he would stir up the muddy bottom and we'd have to wait for the water to settle before we could drink. But this time he was incredibly quiet. Sometimes we would play with him, placing a thin stick in front of him which he grabbed with his pinchers, and we'd lift him out of the water for a minute or so; if we felt exceptionally brave, we would stealthily slip our hand behind the pinchers, around his belly and watch him "paw" at the air until we put him back into his watery home. Our brothers, Paul and Gee Gee had shown us how to do it without getting pinched. Farm kids learned to make every chore contain a little portion of fun time.

And we named all the critters. It made them feel more special to us. This crawdad's name was Crabby Caleb, a good old Bible name.

Frenchie, the frog had been sitting on a rock nearby and decided to wait until we were through drinking before he plopped into the water. Paul and Gee Gee would "gig" for frogs in the creek pond and fry the legs. They tasted like fried chicken. Gigging is done with a spear, and I guess, for boys it was a great pastime, but we girls never wanted to watch this sport.

Rising, we sat on the hillside enjoying the breeze as it rustled through the recently awakened spring leaves. How peaceful it seemed after such a long and traumatic winter when our entire world had collapsed and turned topsy-turvy, upside -down.

We picked some violets, which grew in the shady, damp area surrounding the spring. We would put them in a pint size mason jar to decorate our table at our house down the hill at the end of the path.

"When do you think Daddy's coming back?" I asked my big sister. I always looked up to Patty because she was older than I and I considered her to be so wise. She always had a conclusive answer for all my questions since she was seven and I was only five. She pondered the question while swatting at a stinkbug, which had landed on her foot. "Get off, you stinky old thing," she almost shouted to the unwelcome pest. "I hate those stinky bugs. After you smash'em, you can't get rid of the smell."
Then came her answer, "I don't know. We've waited two days and nights already and no Daddy yet. Can't help but worry

what happened. He said he'd only be gone a few hours and here it is two days already. We've got to figure out a plan in a day or two because we've got to get some food somehow. Our stomachs have already been growling like two old black bears in a fight to the finish." Always practical, Patty was both down to earth and full of imagination and lots of fun to be around. "Do you reckon a bear got 'im?", I asked with shakiness in my voice, which I couldn't hide.

"More likely he got to drinking with Slim and Frosty and forgot what day it is." Patty surmised "or maybe he's looking for work again. One or two days a week just doesn't bring in the bacon. Speaking of bacon, there's a tiny bit left in the smoke house, enough for one more breakfast. It wouldn't be so bad if those darn chickens would start doing their job. That's because they aren't getting enough to eat. I guess hens have to have food to make eggs with."

"Yeah, I guess so. All the crack corn is gone except a mere handful. They're just pecking around for bugs and worms now." I spoke. "I heard somebody say it's okay for them to eat bugs and worms. When they make the eggs, are we eating bugs and worms, too?" I asked.

"No Silly. Somehow God turns all that junk into something that's good when it becomes eggs."

"What I always wondered about is how do they get those big eggs out of their bottoms?"

Patty said, "Well, I don't know, but I'll bet it hurts; that's probably why they squawk and cackle, too." Patty got a good laugh out of that. "Oh, well; I guess we'd better fill our buckets and head down to the house," she said. "At least we've got water to drink and tea bags. Don't know if we have any sugar, but I think there's a little honey left. We can sweeten our tea with that. If only we had a little sugar to make pancakes. I used to watch Mom mix the batter. I know she used flour and sugar, but I don't know what else. Oh, yeah - milk; you have to use milk!

I wondered, "Do you think we can milk Betsy? Her bag is getting full, and she'll be bawling if we don't get that milk out."

"Yeah, I don't think there's much to it, according to what I've seen Gee Gee and Paul do. At least Betsy won't have to haul those two on her back coming to the barn. I don't think it's fair to ride her in and then take her milk."

"Daddy use to tell them not to do that, but we knew they were bound and determined to slip and do it, hoping Mom and Daddy wouldn't see them," Patty ventured.

I whined, "Boy, I sure miss our brothers. We wouldn't be afraid if they were here. They're always doing something stupid, but I guess that's boys for you. But they're always good to us showing us how to do things and explaining things to us. I wish I knew where they are. But I know, wherever they are, God is watching over them because the Bible tells us that Jesus will never leave us or forsake us. I'm so glad Mother reminded us of that before she went to heaven."

"And we've got to remember that, too, when we get afraid," Patty said.

On down the hill we traveled, our bare feet leaving tracks in the sand and dirt. We passed the barn and the chicken house, no cackling there. We could see Betsy down by the creek and knew it shouldn't be hard to catch her and bring her to the barn. We could hear the tinkling sound of her cow bell around her neck as we went into the barn to get her halter, so we could lead her home. Betsy was so gentle. We led her back to the barn and put her in her stall.

By this time, our water buckets were only half full; so much had splashed out on our trek down the hill. The fire had gone out of the kitchen stove while we were gone.

"Let's get a fire started and try to find something to cook for supper. We'll soon have to light the kerosene lamps and wash the lamp shades. We don't want it to get dark before we milk Betsy and feed ol' Dan. He's probably in the stall next to Betsy waiting on his supper." He'd been out eating grass all day. We loved riding ol' Dan. So did Gee Gee and Paul. He was a terrific work horse, with a very gentle and playful spirit.

ALL ALONE WITH CHICKENS, SNAKES, AND SPIDERS

Somehow between Patty trying to do the milking and me trying to console ol' Betsy by petting her and feeding her a handful of feed, we managed to get about two cups of milk from her.

Then we went to the hen house hoping to find some eggs. The dominecker hens (black and white striped) had been doing most of the egg laying for a while, but the Rhode Island reds weren't contributing much to our food supply. We liked to gather the eggs and we always enjoyed petting the hens and talking to them. They made the softest little clucks, when we visited them, except for one old grouchy dominecker. She didn't like for us to reach under her to get her egg (if there were one!) and would squawk and peck at our hands, but we wouldn't give up until we knew whether there was an egg under her. She was especially grouchy that day and Patty gave her a little smack on her backside, and she flew off that nest like a streak of lightning! And glory be! There was one big egg lying there. We named her Daisy after the comic strip character in Lil' Abner.

There were no other eggs and thank goodness ol' Peter-Arnell-Popeye-Guy was lying in the corner sound asleep. That rooster would sometimes attack Patty (they call that flogging), but she pretended not to be afraid of him. He had such a long name because Patty and I kept thinking of names for him and couldn't decide on one, so we named him all these names! Peter Arnell was a news reporter on the radio, and everyone knows who Popeye is and Guy was our uncle's name, Daddy's brother.

We took our precious milk and one egg inside so we could fix us something to eat. We had to build a fire in the kitchen stove. Looking in the wood box behind the stove, we discovered that there was no wood in the box. Oh well, guess we'd better go do some chopping or try to find some dead tree branches or old sticks. So, we went to the wood pile out back to look for some.

All the wood was too long to fit in the fire box. Patty decided to climb on top of the logs for some pieces of tree bark or some small sticks. She found a few and threw them down to me and started her way back down the wood pile. She was close to the bottom when she thought she saw a piece we could use. Suddenly, I let out a scream, "Patty, a snake! " She had almost put her hand on that snake! She tried to jump the rest of the way and fell, while I was going after the axe, so I could kill that awful critter.

By the time I got back there, the ugly rascal was gone. "Thank you, Jesus! " I said when I knew she hadn't been bitten. But I saw blood running down her leg. So, I helped her hobble into the house and into a kitchen chair. I got a washcloth, put soap and water on it and scrubbed her wound. It wasn't really bad, just a small gash below her knee. "Now, I said, somewhere in the cabinet there's a bottle of mercurochrome to help it get better." I looked until I found it, and even though it burned, Patty didn't cry or yell when I poured it on the wound. "I still can't figure out why God made snakes and spiders," I said. "Beats me, said my brave sister, but someday when we get to heaven, we'll ask God or Jesus why they made such awful things."

I went back out and gathered up sticks and branches and brought them in. Patty found the matches, wadded up some paper and carefully stacked the wood on top, then lit the paper.

Soon we had a nice little fire. Patty put on a teakettle of water, found the tea bags and glory be! a little bit of sugar for our tea! We both had to pool our strength to get the big iron skillet on the stove to fry the egg. Boy! What a surprise when Patty cracked that egg, and it had a double yoke! Hooray for good ol' Daisy!

We found some bread in the breadbox and laid it in the skillet to toast it. We also found some strawberry jelly in the cabinet. Soon we were filling our tummies with egg, warm milk, some half-toasted bread, and a hot steaming cup of tea.

Patty said the blessing, "Dear God, please take care of Mommy who is up there with you, and please find our Daddy and send him back to us. Take care of Yvonne and Jerry, Wilma, and Herbert, Gee Gee., and Paul, wherever they are, and please keep us safe from bears and dangerous things until Daddy gets back. And thank you! I didn't get snake bit today. Please help our guardian angel to come to our house tonight. In Jesus name, Amen. "

"Amen," I echoed. "Oh, God; I forgot, thank you for this food and for Betsy and Daisy providing this meal for us. Amen."

After we cleaned up our mess, we gave some pieces of bread to Rex, our dog. "We'd better go to the toilet and get the slop jar and bring it in before it gets dark," I said.

"Yeah, and let's hope Rex sleeps on the back porch tonight." Patty said.

So, we went to the toilet, did our business, and brought back the potty, so we could use it, should the need arise during the night. We decided to move furniture in front of the doors to keep any unwelcome guests from coming in. We pushed everything we could manage against the back and front doors.

"Now, are we going to sleep in our bed upstairs or are we going to sleep down here on the couch?" I asked. "I don't know. I guess we'd feel better in our own bed," Patty said. We already had the kerosene lamps ready, way before dark. We cleaned the glass globes and lit the wicks. We blew out one and Patty carried the other one up the stairs so we could change into our gowns, say our prayers, and get into our bed.

The shadows shining through the window made patterns on the wall and we lay there guessing what they symbolized. Some were scary looking, like spider webs. One looked like a cross, one like a cat, and one like an angel. We heard a sound in the ceiling. We figured it was a squirrel that had found his way up there.

We put our arms around each other and even though it felt lonely and scary, we soon fell asleep for a second night all alone in the log house in the big, dark woods.

WAITING FOR DADDY

Patty and I awoke to a very pretty day. We had slept well. The only animals we heard during the night were dogs in the distance and a coyote somewhere in the woods and that squirrel in the attic, some hoot owls, and our favorite, a lonely whip-poor-will. The hoot owls make such a lonely sound with their who-who, whooo calls. The whip-or-wills sang their lovely, but lonely sounding melodies at twilight. I dearly love to hear their call, even yet.

We enjoyed their music every evening at twilight. Mother had told us to listen to the first call, which was usually the male calling to his mate and the answering call would be that of the female. That always intrigued me, to think that birds sang love songs to each other. Our heavenly Father thought of everything when he made our world and all living creatures, didn't He? The call of the whip-or-will sounds like it is "saying whip-or wheel," "whip-or wheel." Some people use to call this bird a poor Will. Others interpreted their call as if the bird were saying, "Whip poor (Mr.) Will."

When we awakened, we made our bed, dressed, and went downstairs. We moved all the furniture back where it belonged and took the potty out to the toilet to empty and rinse it. We fed the animals with the little food that we had. Patty and I took turns riding around on ol' Dan, bareback. Then we fed the chickens, milked Betsy (got about one cup more milk than yesterday,) got one egg from the chickens, fed Rex and Fluffy, the cat, and went back into the house to fix breakfast.

We built a fire in the cook stove and had the same thing for breakfast that we had yesterday except we added one more item to our menu. Patty decided to make gravy. We had drunk all the milk. We had no refrigerator (no electricity) and took milk and butter up to the spring to keep it cold. So, Patty browned some flour in the skillet then added salt, pepper, and water. Well, the gravy tasted like paste or glue so we gave it to Fluffy and Rex, but they wouldn't eat it either! "Must have been pretty bad if they didn't eat it," I said.

We decided we needed to be good housekeepers 'til Daddy got back, so we swept the downstairs rooms - kitchen, living room, dining room and mopped all three floors. We moved all the furniture, even the heavy couch; we then put it all back and dusted the furniture. We did the dishes, then went upstairs, made all the beds. When the family was intact, everyone slept up there. Yvonne and Wilma slept together, G.G and Paul in a bed in another corner, Patty, and I in our pretty cherry wood bed. Mother and Daddy had a separate area partitioned off with cardboard walls.

It was early afternoon when we finished our work. We played with Rex and Fluffy and made "mud" pies, using jar rings to pat them out. Suddenly, we heard a vehicle coming up the road!

"Oh, goodie," I said. "Daddy's back! "

"No, it's not Daddy." Patty said. "Hear the difference in the sound of the motor? Doesn't sound like Daddy's car." It was a yellow truck - Uncle Guy's truck. He drove into the back yard and stepped out of the truck.

"Hi girls," he said. "I heard you two were up here in this wilderness all alone."

"Well," Patty said, "We're just waiting on Daddy to get back."

"And how long has he been gone?" he asked.

"Today makes the third day," Patty answered. "Seems like a long time to me," I said. "We cleaned up all the house and have everything as clean as a whistle," I said.

"Daddy will like what we did. We even milked the cow but didn't get much milk. Guess Patty doesn't have as much strength in her hands as Gee Gee and Paul. "

"Well," Uncle Guy said, " You two can't stay up here in these woods all by yourself. Your Aunt Maggie and I have decided you need to come down to our house while Sid is gone. He should have never gone off and left you all here like this. I don't know what's gotten into him."

"We're making it just fine," Patty argued, with her arms folded and standing as tall as she could. "We'll stay right here till Daddy comes back," she said.

"Yeah," I added defiantly.

Uncle Guy whipped out a newspaper from his back pocket and said, " You need to see this. "

Unfolding the Beckley Post-Herald newspaper, he pointed to a picture on the front page. There laid our Daddy on a stretcher and two men were putting him into an ambulance!

"Oh, my goodness," I cried, "What's wrong? Is he dead?" Tears were choking up my eyes 'til I could hardly see.

Patty read the description underneath the picture: "Pax man hit by an automobile while crossing Neville Street." She read on. "It doesn't seem that the injuries are serious. Mr. Brunk was held in the Raleigh County Jail due to intoxication for the past forty-eight hours. Mr. Brunk was transported to the Beckley Hospital emergency room for evaluation. "

"What's intoxication?" I asked sniffling and trying to catch my breath.

Uncle Guy said, "It means they put him in jail because he was drunk."

"I've never seen Daddy drunk!" Patty said.

"Well, the newspaper doesn't lie," said Uncle Guy. "Now get your things and let's go."

"Nope, we're not going," Patty said. And with that, she started running toward the chicken house, little sister following closely behind, lickety-split just as fast as we could go!

Now the chicken house was simply perfect for climbing. At each corner, the logs crisscrossed like an x only more like a plus (+) sign. Up those crisscrossed logs went Patty, going so fast you would think her bloomers were on fire! I was doing surprisingly good, too, as fast as Patty. We got up on the roof before Uncle Guy got across the yard. I guess he was slow because he was old, at least forty or fifty - something, I suppose.

The roof was hot, and we had to keep our feet moving so neither of our feet got too terribly hot. Finally, we sat down, our under pants and dress tails between our bottoms and the hot roof.

"You two come down from there! "Uncle Guy shouted.

"Nope," we both yelled. "We're simply fine. We're worried about Daddy, but the paper said it didn't seem like he was injured too badly." Patty said. "And I'm sure, as soon as he's better he'll remember his two littlest girls." I said.

Uncle Guy couldn't climb up the crisscrosses and we wouldn't come down. So, we had reached an impasse.

"Okay," Uncle Guy said, "but I'll be back. Your Aunt Maggie and Grandma Brunk are really worried about you. "

"Tell them we're okay and we must stay here and take care of ol' Dan, Betsy, the chickens, and Rex and Fluffy. Daddy will bring us down to see y'all after he gets home," I said.

"And thanks for coming by." "Yeah," Patty said.

He got into his truck, and we waved bye. "It really was nice to see another person wasn't it," I said.

"Yeah, but he's too snoopy," Patty said.

As soon as he was out of sight, we scampered down off that hot roof, like it was on fire. "Whoo! It's hot up there!" Patty said. We walked across the yard and there laid that newspaper. We stared at it for a while and then we decided our best plan of action was to go down to the creek and play a while and cool off; hunt something to eat and then pray for Daddy to get well and come home.

We loved that creek! It hardly ever got deep. We just sat down and let the gentle stream flow over us. Yvonne, who was a book worm, would often go sit in the creek on a sweltering day and read to her heart's content. We ended up having a good ole water battle. Then, we headed back to the house, thoroughly wet, but well refreshed.

"If I could just remember how to kill and cook a chicken, we'd eat high on the hog this evening," Patty said.

I burst out laughing, "How you gonna eat high on the hog

when it's a chicken?"

We both had a good hearty laugh out of that.

We didn't have chicken for supper. Instead. we went to the garden and pulled up some tiny carrots, radishes, onions, and lettuce and ate that for supper. And I guess we'd have gotten mighty hungry had it not been for Betsy giving us some milk.

Once more we went to bed after praying a long time for Daddy to get well and come home. Will he come home tomorrow?

DADDY COMES HOME

It was cloudy and rainy. We found some books and read awhile and read the Bible some. We liked the Psalms and the things Jesus said in Matthew, Mark, Luke, and John, like "come unto me all ye that labor and are heavy laden and I will give you rest." (Matthew 1, 1:28.) And "Behold the fowls of the air: for they sow not, neither do they reap, nor gather into barns; yet your heavenly Father feedeth them. Are ye not much better than they? "(Matthew 6:26).

I couldn't read well, but I just loved to read. I had been learning for a year. We played around with Mother's organ - one pumping the foot pedals, while the other tried to make a melody on the keys. We went out and got our pet chicken named Blondie and let her walk on the keys. Not much melody there, but a lot of fun. Then we brought Fluffy in and let her "play" a while.

It quit raining in the early afternoon. We were out in the yard playing with Rex and Fluffy when we heard a car coming up the road! We looked at each other and started jumping up and down.

"God heard our prayers, I betcha! " Patty squealed. "I bet it's Daddy!" I loudly squealed. Then we saw the model T come around the bend and down the little slope to the creek.

We both started running and met Daddy before he got half-way up the lane to the house. He stopped the car and jumped out and two little girls climbed up as he reached down to encircle us in his arms.

"How's my girls," Daddy asked.

"Glad to see you! " Patty said, almost crying.

I was hanging onto his neck crying and blubbering like a baby. Then I snuffed and sniffled and wiped my eyes (and nose) on my dress sleeve. In a muffled and slightly shaky voice, I said, "Daddy, we missed you! Where in the world did you go and leave us all alone? We were so lonesome and scared!"

Daddy looked so ashamed. He reminded me of Rex when somebody would scold him, very sheepish - like. "I did something wrong and I'm sorry" he said. "Most of all I'm sorry that I left you two here all alone. I promise I'll never do that again." "We know all about it," Patty said, "How you got drunk and got put in jail." "And then got hurt and went to the hospital." I piped up.

"How'd you know all that? He asked. "God told us" Patty said.

"No, He didn't," I said. "Uncle Guy came here yesterday to take us home with him to Grandma's house. And he brought a Beckley Newspaper and we saw your picture and we thought you were dead!"

"We read the piece in the paper, and they said they were taking you to the hospital," Patty said. She had tears running down her face and she cried," We were so scared that you would die like Mom did, and then we would have nobody. We'd be orphans!" At this point she was bawling like I'd never seen her cry. "But we wouldn't go with Uncle Guy," I added. Dad dried our tears with his handkerchief.

He was so ashamed. "Well, I'm all healed up and we'll try to forget these last few days and start all over. Things will get better, I'm sure. Look in the car. I bought some groceries and there's a treat in there for you. "

We climbed down off Daddy and got into the car and rode the rest of the way to the house. We were happy to see food! And he brought us each a bag of penny candy and suckers (lollipops.)

We were two happy girls again! It felt so good to have our Daddy home. We didn't know it then, but our lives were to change drastically within a few months, but nothing would ever be as bad as it was on December 13, 1940. That was the day our entire world fell apart and nothing would ever put it back together again.

Nothing would ever be the same.

GOLDEN RIBBON DEC 1940

I awoke from a deep, revitalizing sleep, shivering with excitement. Was it a dream I had experienced? If so, I had dreamed it before. But it seemed so real! I could remember every detail, just as if I had truly experienced every single event! The past ten days had seemed like a horrible nightmare. We all walked around like we were living in a deep, dark fog. It seemed as if hope was gone, and loneliness and emptiness had taken its place. Christmas was about a week away, but no one had the heart to do anything that we normally did to celebrate Christ's birthday. We tried to fight off the lethargy that had overtaken us. We somehow managed to do the daily tasks that, but without any joy. Our darling Mother who lived only for her family was GONE! She had been only thirty-eight years old when the cancer took her life.

How to celebrate Christmas, when all the light and love had gone out of our lives? Daddy had fallen apart. Their love had been so great and now the love of his life was gone, was his reason for living. The older children tried to help him, to no avail. He mostly slept. When Patty and I climbed up on his lap and put our little arms around him and reminded him that Mother was with Jesus and the angels, in a beautiful place, with no more pain, he seemed to "perk up" a little.

I remember him lying on the couch, and Patty and I got some

cellophane paper pieces and ran a comb through his hair, then held it near the bits of cellophane and they would "jump" onto the comb. This was great fun and a comfort to him. In the dimness of the room, we could see sparks created by the static electricity. Daddy had taught us about that phenomenon. He was always teaching us unusual things. He was quite an inventive person, even though he only had an eighth-grade education.

Jerry and Herbert came almost every evening to "court" Yvonne and Wilma and Herbert often brought his guitar and played beautiful songs. The four of them would make taffy and candy in the kitchen. Sometimes they would pay Patty and me to make ourselves scarce so they could be alone with their sweethearts. Their nickels and dimes added up to a candy bar or bottle of "pop" every now and then. And Herbert's sticks of chewing gum always hit the spot.

Being so young, I could not grasp the meaning of death. Why did God need Mother more than we did? I tried to understand, but no one really wanted to talk about it. A feeling of heavy sadness permeated the air.

One night, I went to bed longing for my Mommy and started crying. I finally got up and looked out the attic window and looked for Mother in the stars.

I knew heaven was up there somewhere. Was she lying in that Big Dipper? Daddy and Mother had told us about the Big and Little Dipper, the Milky Way, Orion, the Lion, Leo, and others. Was she in that group called the Lion? I hoped not, because I didn't like lions. The Big Dipper seemed friendlier, so I pretended she was curled up asleep in that dipper. But it was so far away, and I couldn't reach it! The family told me she was in Heaven. But was the Big Dipper in Heaven? I didn't think so. But where was she?

Looking up at the stars, I decided that I'd find a way to get to her, some way, somehow, some day! Each night, I looked out that window and asked Jesus to take me to her or to bring her back to us. I sensed that He couldn't bring her back to us. So, it was up to me and Jesus to find out how I could go to her. I felt better already!

Christmas in 1940, was now only a week away. Everyone was trying to get some semblance of a Christmas spirit, but only half-heartedly. I didn't want anything for Christmas but my Mother. Now, I had heard about fairies, make-believe stories, and real-live angels in the Bible.

Being an avid reader already, I'd take the few books we owned and hide away under the stairway (my favorite place) with my doll, Marguerite, who Mother had made for me last year. I would read to my doll and explain to her about Heaven, Jesus, what little I knew about dying and sing a song to her that Mother had sung to me.

Here I was, rocking back and forth, comforting my dolly, and telling her we would find a way to make Christmas come alive somehow. I just couldn't let the joy of Christmas fade into nothing-ness! That night, I lay in bed thinking and looking out the window. Could I write a message to Mother and address it to God or the angels and tell them to let me know that Mother was safe, warm, free of pain, well-fed and happy and could she let me know these things?

So, the next day, with pencil and paper in hand, Marguerite and I went into our private little closet and began a letter to Heaven.

Dear God, A few weeks ago, your angels came and got my Mother and took her to Heaven. Have you seen her? She's the lovely lady with sparkling brown eyes, dark brown hair-almost black, always a smile and a song. She's very smart, loves music, dancing, flowers, kittens, dogs and most of all, Daddy and us Kids.

Do you celebrate Christmas there? If so, would you please give her a gift from us? She loves anything you give her, like perfume (she always smelled good), a poem, or a song, a good joke, Milky Way and Baby Ruth candy bars, dancing, flowers and most of all, good hugs.

Please answer my letter as soon as possible because Christmas is almost here; and the best gift you could give me, God, is to let me know she isn't sick now and is happy.

I'll be watching for your letter.

Love,
Ailene

P.S. We don't have a real post office address here, but we live in the log house at the end of the road where the beautiful mountain laurels grow, just past that big, moss-covered rock in the path. It's a muddy road in winter, but you can skate across the creek and it's only a hop and a skip to our house.

P.S. again - I'll leave a yellow hankie hanging beneath my upstairs window by the big tree.

Now, just how do you get a letter to heaven? I thought a long time and, as usual, when I need an answer, I went to Patty. She's maybe a little smarter than me, although she was scared of cows, and I was not. I walked her to school past the cows in the mornings and came back home alone. Rex, our dog, went to get her in the evenings.

Well, Patty did have an idea as she always did! She said, "You know we always made our list out to Santa and then threw it into the fireplace. When it burned to a cinder, the wind would pick it up and blow it to the North Pole. It had always worked. We always got something for Christmas no matter how little the gift. So, we made sure the fire was hot and dropped the letter in. We watched it burn to a crisp and prayed that the wind would pick it up and take it straight to God in heaven. It was our only hope. It made it up through the chimney at least.

That night we looked out the window and prayed to Jesus to take my letter to God and read it to him. I knew somehow the letter would make it through to God. Each night we prayed hard, and, for good measure, Marguerite and I prayed several times a day in our secret place. Well, it was now only two days until Christmas, and I was getting anxious.

We wrapped up in our winter clothes and went out to look through the snow to see if the letter from God was anywhere out there. We went down to the creek, and because it was frozen, we skated across and then went on down the road, scaring an owl, who screeched at us and went on down to the moss-covered rock. That is where Daddy, Mother and Yvonne often took us, and we could watch the sunset and sing "Red Sails in the Sunset" and other good songs.

When it began to get dark, we decided we had to go back to the house. We got up and with a lack of our usual light heartedness and humor, started to go back home.

"Just two more days, Ailene. Do you suppose we will ever hear from God by then," said Patty?

"Sure, I said. "God wants his kids to have a joyous Christmas. I'm sure He got my letter and will answer it some way. We just must keep praying and believing."

We made our little paper chains and did our best to hang pretty Angels on the tree with loving messages to our family. We made popcorn and strung it on the string (except for the part that we ate). We made paper chains, too. Everything we put on the tree made it prettier.

Christmas Eve came. No letter from God had arrived. We

knelt by our bed, clasped each other's hands, and looked up at the star-studded sky. The windows were all white and frosty and we prayed our prayer as usual.

We climbed into our bed. Suddenly, we could hear a high, crystal-clear voice singing a song mother had sung to us. It was a song she herself had written! She had only sung it to Patty and me when we were trying to go to sleep. The title of the song was, "We Always Live Within Each Other's Hearts."

The voice was singing loudly, and we scampered out of bed to look out the window. Down at the creek was a figure who was skating around on the ice. Was it Wilma or Yvonne? They often skated on the creek, but never at night. But no, it couldn't be them, they were sound asleep in their bed.

Who was the mysterious person skating and easily gliding about ever so perfectly, singing with beautiful symphonic music accompanying her? We knew it was a girl or a lady because of her clear soprano voice. Louder it rang over the snow-covered hills and valleys.

We decided God had sent an Angel to bring us a message from heaven! The Angel skated and sang this beautiful song:

> *We always live within each other's hearts,*
> *There's nothing that can tear our love apart.*
> *We live our lives till it is time to go,*
> *But when we leave, we all must know*
> *That where one goes, we all can go.*

And someday, live and laugh,
And play, and dance, and sing, and shout, and say,
That death can never make us bend,
And love that knows no bounds can't end.
So, keep this message in your heart,
And know we're never far apart.
I'm just beyond the rainbow's end,
Where we, my darlings, meet again.
Keep your love strong, be gentle and kind,
And spread good cheer to all mankind.
Keep trusting God, lean on His breast,
And when you're weary, He'll give you a rest.
Read His word and watch and pray,
And keep Him close day by day.
Then someday when your work is done,
His Angels will gently lead you home.
I'll be the first one you'll embrace,
And be so glad to see your face!
I love you more than words can say
And I'll be waiting for you on that day!

The Angel continued skating and singing that familiar song over several more times. She had a curious glow about her. Her white gown was made of something like the gossamer wings of a butterfly. She skated like her feet were off the ground. She had a wide Golden Ribbon around her waist which swayed as she whirled around and around. Finally, she whirled up, up and away through the clouds, until we could see her no more.

We were as astounded as the shepherds had been on that

first Christmas night long ago. The glow of it all lingered. We marveled in "oohs and ahhs" over what we had seen and heard. We believed that God had answered our prayers in this unusual way. We couldn't go to sleep; we were so excited! Finally, we climbed into bed and drifted off to a peaceful sleep and dreamland.

Next morning, we awoke to find a beautifully decorated tree and cookies and gingerbread men. There was a child sized table, set with a beautiful set of China dishes. There was a little sewing machine for Patty which really sewed and a little washing machine for me. Seated at the table was a pretty doll sitting on one of the child-sized chairs. She had light brown hair and beautiful brown eyes. In another chair, sat a pretty, blonde-headed doll with blue eyes. Patty's name was written on the arm of the brown-haired doll and my name was written on the arm of the blonde headed one. Around the waist of each doll was a wide diaphanous Golden Ribbon! We thought Mother had sent this lovely Christmas to us since she couldn't be here herself. It is all still a great mystery to us, and I guess we will never know for sure where it all came from. What a precious, special Christmas memory!

"AFTER MOTHER PASSED"

Now that our dear mother had gone to heaven, a place had to be found for Patty and me. We lived some with Daddy at our home place up in Brunk Hollow, but I know we lived in separate places sometimes after mother left. We lived for a little while with Mother's sisters, Aunt Laura Teel, Aunt Lottie Cole, and Aunt Macil Brunk.

Patty lived with mother's oldest sister, Aunt Laura Pittman Teel who lived at the bottom of Grandpa's hill in Sprague, WV. During that time, I lived with Aunt Lottie Pittman Cole, who lived across town on Bailey Avenue. It was only about two or

DOROTHY, RUTH, MATTIE,
LOTTIE AND LAURA

three miles from one house to the other, but I don't remember knowing that Patty was living just a few short miles from me.

Patty didn't stay long at Aunt Laura's house. Aunt Laura was the oldest of Grandpa and Grandmother's children. Aunt Laura had a big family and Patty told me one cousin, Dale Teel, was especially nice to her. Cousin Susie was closest to Patty's age, a year or two older.

Patty then went to live with Aunt Macil and Uncle Roy Brunk who lived on Hargrove Street, which was about one and a half miles from where I was but neither she nor I knew where the other was for some time. She was incredibly happy there. They had a baby grand piano to play, and Joy played the violin in the school band. Aunt Macil was a nurse at Beckley Hospital. Uncle Roy had been injured in World War II and could not work.

When I lived with Aunt Lottie Cole, I didn't often see Uncle Fred Cole, Aunt Lottie's husband. Uncle Fred was also a member of the Brunk family. He was Daddy's sister Lillie's son. So, their daughter Jewel and I were first cousins because Aunt Lottie and mother were sisters and Uncle Fred was Daddy's nephew. So, we were also second cousins.

My cousin Jewel often took me for walks. I really liked her. Years later, she moved to Baltimore and became a nurse. I really looked up to her. Her sister, Margie Meade, lived on Bailey Avenue about a mile away. Her husband Jack died in World War II. I remember Jewel and Margie taking me to their church, the regular Baptist church on Johnstown Road. How long were Patty and I at these temporary homes? I don't know. I would say it was probably a few months.

Then we returned to our own home up in Brunk Hollow about a mile from the town of Pax, West Virginia. I loved our log cabin in the Hollow. Mother had planted flowers all around our house. We had several acres which Daddy, Paul, and G.G tended. We raised almost all our own food. It was a happy time in the Hollow until Mother died. When she went away our sunshine was gone.

We loved living with mother's sisters. Aunt Laura lived down at the end of the road that went to Grandfather's Grand House. It was where the road ended at the junction with Beckley's main thoroughfare which used to be called Valley Drive. The road was later renamed "Robert C. Byrd Drive" and goes all the way from Blue Ridge Memorial Gardens near Mt. Hope (where some of our relatives are buried) all the way to Sophia (on the south side of town) and goes on to Mullens in Wyoming County.

Patty wasn't there very long. Aunt Macil and Uncle Roy took her to their house. She was happy there. We lived a few months at mother's sisters' houses. It's hard to know about time when you are a kid. Most of this book comes from my memories of things between the ages of two and five. It is only through the grace of God that I can remember things that happened in my life at such an early age.

I have had a longing in my heart for years to write about our family and the impact that losing a parent can have upon a child. It was devastating for our family, and I have missed Mother, and later Daddy, all these years. But the grace of God is marvelous. Father Jehovah saw that we were taken care of for the few days we were alone when Daddy was gone.

It was such a devastating time for all the kids. Yvonne had Jerry to help her through her grieving process and Wilma had Herbert to help with her grief. My brothers, Gee Gee and Paul, set out to work and stayed in a variety of places. Paul went to work for a farmer in Ghent, a town about halfway between Beckley and Princeton. He stayed at Aunt Lottie's house for a brief time while I was living there.

Gee Gee got a job at Beckley Feed and Hardware delivering ice to people in the local area. He would later tell us that he had a unique test to get that job. The owner put a block of ice on the floorboard and Gee Gee had to prove that he could operate the truck without moving the big block of ice! He would later go on to work at various farms in the West Virginia and Virginia area for about two years. He was always mysterious about where and who he worked for during that time.

But those days alone in Brunk's Hollow were scary for Patty and me. We just could not understand where Daddy was until Uncle Guy came over and showed us the newspaper with Daddy's picture. They were placing him into the ambulance. We were afraid and tired, and we were missing our family.

LIVING WITH TWO OF MOTHER'S SISTERS - 1941

I went to live with Mother's sister, Aunt Lottie, and her husband Fred Cole on Bailey Ave near Pinecrest Tuberculosis Sanatorium. Aunt Lottie's daughter, Jewel, was a cousin whom I felt close to. She would take me to the Beckley Regular Baptist Church. Jewel has always been close to me and to all my sisters, especially Yvonne. She was always an inspiration to me.

Aunt Macil Pittman was Mother's sister, and her husband Uncle Roy was Daddy's brother. Their daughters Joy and Dorothy were their two children. Uncle Roy married Macil Pittman

UNCLE ROY AND AUNT MACIL

and his brother Sidney, our father, married our mother, Lillian Pittman.

We were quite close to Joy and now her daughter, Barbara Jo and her husband, Gene Byrd of North Carolina. The family of Senator Robert C. Byrd raised Gene Byrd. Barbara and I talk with each other about every week or two over the phone. We both love the Lord, His word, and His church. We have had many discussions about the Bible, the condition of the world and our dear country.

I loved staying at Aunt Lottie's house and Patty loved to be at Aunt Macil's and Uncle Roy's. I don't know how long we were at these two relative's homes. But I guess Daddy had something to do with us going to Aunt Maggie's next.

LIVING WITH GRANDMA BRUNK, AUNT MAGGIE AND UNCLE GUY (1941-46)

Sometime before the school year started in 1941, Patty and I went to live at Grandma Brunk's (Nancy Margaret Clemens Brunk) house and I started school at Pax Elementary School in Pax, Fayette County, West Virginia.

I don't remember how we ended up living at Grandma Brunk's house which was situated high on a hill in the little town of Pax. Did Daddy take us there? Did someone else take us there? I remember nothing at all about that transition. There is no one older than I who could tell me that except Patty and she doesn't know either.

Grandma Brunk lived there with her daughter and bachelor son,
(Aunt Maggie (Maggie A. Shepherd) and Uncle Guy (John Guy Brunk). Grandpa Brunk (John Griffith Brunk) died in 1933 and Aunt Maggie moved in with Grandma and Uncle guy to run the household and take care of Grandma, who was then seventy-six years old. She also had a good memory. If anyone asked her how old a certain grandchild was, she could tell them right on the money.

I think her favorite grandchild was my brother, Paul, who came to visit often. I do not know where he and Gee Gee lived, maybe up in Brunk Hollow. Nobody knew where our Daddy was, just traveling the country, I guess. We would only see him once or twice a year when he came to see us all.

One time Daddy brought Patty and me a doll and each of us a headscarf. My doll had blonde curly hair like mine and Patty's had light brown hair like hers. I named mine Marguerite. She was just 16-inches tall and beautiful. If Daddy stayed two days, we spent as much time as we could from doing chores to sit on his lap, walk in the yard, sing with him, and comb his hair. It was always like heaven when he came back, and we always went somewhere away from the house to be together. When he left, it broke our hearts, and we cried. We couldn't understand why he could not stay there with us. We never knew where he was going. The truth of it all is he may not have known either. I heard at one time he worked at a florist in Florida.

Recently, I learned why we ended up at Aunt Maggie's. It was during one of our annual Pittman reunions in Beckley that our cousin Betty Bostick Williams told us that after our mother died, Betty asked her mother, Aunt Mattie Bostick, if they could adopt Patty so she could be Betty's sister.

She reminded her mother that they had already discussed that, and Aunt Mattie and Uncle Herman were willing to adopt Patty. Aunt Mattie and Uncle Herman and their children, Ray, the twins Marvin and Melvin, and Betty had moved in with Grandpa Pittman after Grandmother Pittman had died in 1938. They went there to take care of Grandfather. He could no longer take care of the cow, horses, goats, chickens, garden, and house, so having Aunt Mattie there was part of the solution.

As I wrote earlier, it was a large house with 12 or more rooms, and a large yard and garden. There were fireplaces in every room. It was a big place to keep up and it took a lot of people and a lot of work

So, according to Cousin Betty, Patty was her choice for a sister. Betty had put up with her brothers long enough and now was her chance to get the sister she always wanted and loved. Betty was also our favorite cousin. But fortunately, for us, her plan did not work out.

Those six years at Aunt Maggie's were good and bad years for both of us. I will try to explain the ambivalence so the reader will not get a bad opinion of our Aunt Maggie. Both Yvonne and Wilma had married their husbands in 1941 and lived near the town of Pax. They would come over to see us when they could. We always thought that Aunt Maggie was not very friendly to them.

They would ask us to come to their house to see their new babies. Yvonne and Jerry had a little boy named Ronald Calvin Stover and Wilma and Herbert had a little girl named Lana Joy Turner. Ronald was born May 31st and Joy was born on June 18th of the same year.
Sometimes in order to go see our sisters and their families,

Patty and I would go to put roses on Grandpa's grave which wasn't far from where Yvonne lived. We always had to hurry so Aunt Maggie would not know we had gone to Yvonne's.

Sometimes, Aunt Maggie sent us to the Long Branch Company store to buy boiling beef and Wilma lived nearby. We would run as fast as we could down the railroad track one mile to go to the store and then go visit Wilma and Joy for a few minutes. Yvonne and Wilma always gave us something to eat and spoiled us with candy bars, soda pop or something we usually did not get at Aunt Maggie's.

Yvonne and Wilma would tell us much later in life that they bought or sent things for us at Christmas, but we never saw them. We never knew what happened to those gifts. Usually at Christmas time, Aunt Hattie's daughter Chlora, who lived in Hialeah, Florida and had Greyhound race dogs, would send us stuff like fruit and clothes for Christmas. We had permission to have those and school supplies.

Daddy's sister, Aunt Flossie and her family lived in Grants Pass, Oregon. They grew walnuts and she always sent big bags of walnuts to us at Christmas time. We all could enjoy them. Many years later, Arnold and I went to see our cousins in Oregon with Wilma and Herbert. We met them for the first time in all those years.

Christmas time was usually an exciting time even at Aunt Maggie's. She always made a fresh coconut cake, and it was always delicious. We cracked coconuts and shredded the moist coconut with a shredder and Aunt Maggie would make her famous, coconut cake. Yum, Yum.

A few weeks before Christmas, Patty and I would go to the woods and hunt for a Christmas tree. If we couldn't find one, we would find a long stalk and cut branches off other pine trees. Then we would tape them onto the stalk and make us a semblance of a Christmas tree. Aunt Maggie had a box of old decorations and tinsel and one string of lights with bulbs shaped like an egg with pictures on them. We would pray over those lights and if they didn't work, we swapped the eight or nine bulbs around to get them to burn. If that didn't work, we would shake the cord trying to jiggle them into working. Usually, we prayed some more and finally got them to work. When they finally worked, we were so happy!

We did not hang stockings up. We sat our caps on the mantle hoping Santa would come and fill them up with delicious goodies. One night, I woke up and there was Patty filling all the caps with nuts, candy, oranges, apples, and whatever was available. My cap was blue, and Patty's was brown. I never let Patty know I had seen her putting those joyous gifts into our caps. On Christmas morning, we sat around and were thankful that Santa had visited our humble home and filled all our caps. I was grateful to Santa but even more grateful for a sister who always took care of me.

The house only had four rooms; a kitchen, dining room and two bedrooms, one which we called the living room. This was Grandma's and Aunt Maggie's bedroom, and Patty and I slept in a half-bed there, also.

My Grandpa Brunk was a short, small man whose name was John Griffith Brunk. I was told that in one neighborhood, the neighbors had nicknamed them Mr. and Mrs. Tom Thumb. Grandpa died in 1933, the year Patty was born, so we never knew him. Grandma's family had originally lived in Blacksburg, Virginia and later her family moved to the Whitesville, West Virginia area.

Aunt Maggie Brunk, born in 1881, was one of the oldest children in Grandma's family. In those days, the older children took care of the younger ones. There were twelve children in the family, eight girls and four boys. My Daddy Sidney was born in 1897 and was the last of twelve children in his family. Down through the years, we had heard that Grandma Brunk had a relative out West whose name was Samuel Clemens. Author Mark Twain's real name was Samuel Clemens, but I never got around to doing the genealogy, so his connection to our family remains a mystery.

Aunt Maggie used to tell us that our Daddy worked in the mines at the age of seven. She said he picked off the big lumps of coal off the conveyor belt and let the "slack" roll on. She said he would come home in the evening crying with his little hands aching and she would put Vaseline on them and wrap them with cloths. Aunt Maggie was a hard taskmaster, but she had a good heart.

Daddy was always a diligent worker throughout his life. When we were together as a family, he worked in the coal mines, which was a hard job back in those days. He never had more than an eighth-grade education, but he was an intelligent man, and he was quite inventive. He could fix anything. He and mother loved to read. My sisters told me they got my name from the book that they were reading. Daddy was one of the men who paved the way for life to become easier for working men by helping form the union which was called the United Mine Workers of America. That union is still in existence. He was the treasurer of the union.

Patty and I have always been so close. She wrote three books. One was a children's book, "The Boy Who Loved Family Hugs." Another book was a true story of a cruise ship scam called "Sweet Dreams- Bitter Awakenings." She had all three books published. She wrote one called "Patty's Promise" about our life together.

We didn't see our Daddy often. He would surprise us all and come visit maybe once a year. He would always bring Patty and me something. I do know Daddy finally ended up in Wilmington, DE where Gee Gee, Rada and their family lived. Once he sent me a postcard telling me that he was in Saint Mary's hospital in Huntington, West Virginia for removal of a cancerous lung.

Life with Aunt Maggie was hard. I was five or six and Patty was seven or eight when we went there to live. We had to bring in the coal for the two fireplaces and two stoves, carry water from the well and drinking water from our neighbors, the Thompsons. Patty had to stay home every Monday for one-half of the day to do all the washing and laundry.

School started at 9:00 AM and we could never leave on time to walk to school. We left about 5 minutes to 9 and went flying down our hill, crossing the little town of Pax and walked up 102 steps to the school on top of the opposite hill. Sometimes we were tardy. We had two cousins who were teachers there, Beulah Fraser and Chlora Tyree. Beulah paddled me once because I was trying to catch a bus and go to Aunt Hattie Brunk. I didn't know which bus I was supposed to go on, so when they called out the first bus I left, afraid I'd miss my bus, but it was the wrong one. The next morning, Beulah gave me a hard paddling in front of the class. She was mean to me and to this day I don't know why. Life was hard, but my greatest joy was going to school. I wanted so badly to learn.

Grandma Brunk didn't do anything while we lived there except sit in her rocking chair and knit. She would knit a small square about 6 inches square, then she would unravel it and start all over again. At mealtime, Patty and I would each get hold of one of her arms and walk her to the dining room table to eat. When she was through, we would take her back to her rocking chair and get her the two sticks of teaberry gum which she kept in the built-in closet. Since there was no bathroom, she used a portable potty chair. It was our job to carry the "slop jar" (another name for the potty jar) to the toilet to empty it and rinse it out.

Occasionally, we would take a fine-tooth comb and comb out Grandma's long white hair and tie it up into a bun on top of her head. Grandma was good with numbers and could tell you the dates of all her children's and grandchildren's births. She was only about four feet tall. She looked even shorter because or her bent over.

One time Uncle Guy got angry with Patty when she fed the horses. The horse kept raking its fore foot around and she thought it wanted more food, so she fed it more. When Uncle Guy found this out, he was so angry! We had never seen him that angry. He screamed, "If that horse gets sick, I'll whip you within an inch of your life! I'll wear out that horse's bridle on you!"

We got so scared; we ran away. We ran down over the hill where we stopped to catch our breath. Finally, we hid in a ravine for a long time. Someone came out to the top of the hill and yelled, "If you girls don't come back, we are going to get the police after you!" We got so scared again and went right back home. Fortunately for us, Uncle Guy had cooled down and the horse didn't get sick at all. So, we got through that one.

One time Patty and I went through the cornfield, crawled through the barbed wire fence and over to Ray and Ardith Thompson's to pull water out of the well. Usually, we would hurry there and back so we'd have a little time to play with the Thompson boys. There were four of them, Conway, David, Dennis, and Jackie. Jackie was my age, and he was my first love. He was so good to me. They had bikes, scooters, and sleds. They taught us how to use all of them. One day we stayed too long, and Aunt Maggie came to the garden fence and yelled at us to come home. She had switches and we were carrying big water buckets, so it gave her plenty of time to switch us good on the way back.

As I was trying to get through the barbed wire with her switching me, I tore about a seven-inch Y-shaped hole in my left thigh. This time Patty did the medical work on me. She used peach leaf poultices and it healed well. But I still have a large seven-inch scar on my left thigh. One other time, I was riding Jackie Thompson's sled down our Hill and landed in Mrs. Hatfield's fence and cut a Y-shaped gap in my left eyebrow. There is still a scar there, but Aunt Maggie never knew about that one.

CHILDHOOD AT AUNT MAGGIE'S – HER CURE FOR DISOBEDIENCE

Aunt Maggie always punished us with a switch to our legs. Patty was inclined to argue with Aunt Maggie and was quite bold with her. About every day, it seems, she would give us a switching for some little infraction.

How well I remember the day that Patty and I were doing the dishes in the two dish pans on the kitchen table. The table was

NANCY MARGARET BRUNK (SEATED) WITH FLOSSIE, FANNIE, CLARA, HATTIE AND MAGGIE

a sturdy homemade wooden one with an oilcloth tablecloth. Patty was washing and I was drying. We had a pretty, white bowl with blue stars which Aunt Maggie really liked. We had gotten it out of a box of Quaker oats. Well, while washing it, the bowl slid out of Patty's wet soapy hands, hit the floor, and broke into what I thought was a million pieces. Aunt Maggie heard the crash and came to the kitchen to find her cherished bowl on the floor all broken to smithereens. (Smithereens is an old-fashioned word that we used often.) She got so angry and got a large switch which she always seemed to have on hand. She started switching Patty's poor little legs. Patty was hopping around trying to get away from Aunt Maggie and the switch. While doing so she kept stepping in the slivers of glass, which were quite numerous, and as a result, her poor feet were cut and bleeding badly.

But it didn't seem to bother Aunt Maggie that Patty's feet were cut and bloody. We had to clean up the mess, empty the dish pans and finish our work. After Aunt Maggie left the room, I helped Patty hobble to the barn where she laid down. I took a needle and picked the slivers of glass out of her bleeding feet. I found an empty feed sack, tore it into a rag bandage and wrapped her bleeding and swollen feet. Then she hobbled back to the house. I don't even remember Aunt Maggie commenting about it. In fairness to Aunt Maggie, her way of raising us may have come from the way her parents raised her.

When we got back to the house, I gathered leaves off the peach tree and began to squeeze and break them up until juice came out of them. Then I poured salt on the leaves, mixed it up good and placed the poultice on Patty's injured feet and wrapped them with a clean cloth. We had seen Aunt Maggie do this many times when we had stepped on a nail or some other sharp object. The peach tree leaves drew the infections out.

I used to have lots of boils and Aunt Maggie would make an oatmeal poultice. She just made plain old oatmeal, let it cool down some, placed it on the boil and wrapped a rag around it. If that didn't work, she would place a piece of fat back bacon on the boil (or a festered splinter, etc.) and wrapped it. It usually worked.

When we had a chest cold or flu, she made a concoction for a cure. I'm not sure what was in it, but I know it had grease and turpentine in it. She kept it sitting on the fireplace hearth to keep it warm and she sat up all night taking care of us. So, you see she wasn't all bad.

Patty would occasionally walk on the one-inch board that kept the hogs in. But one day she fell in, and you should have seen her! She was a mess! So, we got out that big old, galvanized round tub, poured in some water and she took a bath. At Aunt Maggie's, bathing usually wasn't done until Saturday night. When winter came, we weren't allowed to wash our hair until warm weather came in the springtime. We hated this with a passion. We couldn't figure out why we couldn't be like the other girls who washed their hair every few days.

But Aunt Maggie had her ways. One day she and Patty got into it and Aunt Maggie told Patty to go get two switches off the plum tree. Patti yelled, "I don't care if you bring the whole tree in." Aunt Maggie about wore herself out switching Patty that day. I told Patty if she would quit arguing with her, it wouldn't go so badly with her when she got her whippings. But she never learned. That day she cried and screamed so loudly, the neighbors heard her and asked what had happened. The neighbors knew we had a hard life at Aunt Maggie's.

Sometimes Grandma felt sorry for us and would tell us to get two pieces of teaberry gum out of the chifforobe. It doesn't sound like much, but it helped soothe some of our pain. Grandma sat in her rocking chair all the time in what we called the living room. It was really a bedroom. Patty and I went to bed all huddled up with our arms wrapped around each other. This is how we always slept.

If a person would stop and think of all the burdens laid upon Aunt Maggie's shoulder, a person could not think too badly of her. Children were raised quite differently in those days. Grandma and Grandpa Brunk had twelve children. Aunt Maggie was one of the older ones. I'm sure she had to work hard to help raise them all.

When she grew to womanhood, she married a nice man named Paris Shepherd. Mr. Shepherd was struck by a car and suffered a broken neck. Aunt Maggie took care of him for seventeen years. They never had children. She later came to live with Grandma, Grandpa and Uncle Guy. She took care of Grandpa until he died. To add to her burden of taking care of others, Daddy dropped off two little girls, ages 5 and 7. I should think she had had her fill of taking care of people. Patty and I stayed with Aunt Maggie from around 1941 to 1946.

Patty and I had a lot of work to do. We helped with the cooking, washed the dishes, fed the animals; the horse, chickens, and the pigs; carried in the day's supply of wood, coal, and water. We made beds and cleaned the house, swept, and dusted. Aunt Maggie had asthma bad, so she couldn't be around dust, flour, etc. She would put a wet cloth around her mouth and head, then we would stir up the biscuits and add the buttermilk. Then she would knead them. The biscuits were so good. She was a good cook.

We had to get up incredibly early every morning and get the chores done, get ready for school and take off flying down the hill through town and up 102 steps to the school located on the opposite hill from ours. We left a few minutes before 9:00am and got there just as the bell was ringing most of the time. Charles Nelson Williams and I were the two top students in our first-grade class, but I didn't pass first grade because I broke my right arm and the teacher held it against me because I couldn't write well with my left hand. I always thought that was wrong when I did everything else exceptionally good. But that's the breaks.

FRIENDS WE MADE AT AUNT MAGGIE'S

My best friend was Faye Billups. She was always so nice to me. We played together. She made my life much happier. I admired her because she sang with her mom and dad and sister at the Church of God. They had a good quartet. I see her around here every now and then. I will never forget her kindness.

Another dear friend was my next-door neighbor, Jackie Thompson. We got water from the Thompson's well for drinking and carried it from their house through our cornfield to our house. Jackie would let Patty and me ride his scooter, taught us how to ride his bike, and let us use his sled for sledding in the winter. We had to rush through the cornfield, draw the water, play for a few minutes and rush back home.
I guess Aunt Maggie always timed us because sometimes we took up too much time playing, and she whipped us all the way home.

Jackie's father, Ray Thompson, was an elder or deacon at our church - the Church of Christ at Pax. Aunt Maggie got us started going to the church the family was always connected with. No one at our house went except Patty and me. Grandma couldn't walk, Aunt Maggie wasn't able and as far as I know, Uncle Guy never went. He was a nice person, but he drank a lot, and the town had several "beer joints" which he frequented.

Ray Thompson was our Sunday school teacher, and he sure was a good one! Clint Lively was also one of our teachers. We went to Sunday School, Sunday morning Church, Sunday night service and Wednesday night Bible Study-prayer meeting.

Ray and his wife Ardith had five sons: Conway, David, Dennis, Jackie, and Tommy. They were always kind to us - real Christians - I called them. Jackie was my idol, I guess you could say. I claimed him as my boyfriend though only Patty knew that. She liked Dennis -- he was her age. We were so thankful that they were our friends.

The only other friend we had was Patty's friend Leona Shamblin and Little Pee Wee, who was younger than us, but she came to our house to play. Pee Wee's Dad and Uncle Guy were good friends.
There were the two black boys who lived down the hill from us with their Grandma. We called her Aunt Ella. Our favorite thing to do with them was to get in an old 50-gallon barrel with one of the boys and go flying down the hill rolling and laughing.

Aunt Ella always showed up to help us when we were busy canning. We canned green beans (hundreds of quarts), peaches (50 quarts), blackberries which Patty and I picked, and we made lots of pints of blackberry jelly, cherries for pies and cherry preserves. We had peach, apple, and cherry trees. We made jelly or preserves from all these fruits. Our place provided all the food we ate except for sugar, flour, peanut butter, cereal, Ivory Soap, Rinso, bluing, baking powder, soda and salt and horse feed.

Aunt Hattie Tyree (Daddy's sister) lived about 1-1/2 miles from us. We walked up there once or twice a week. We got milk, buttermilk, and butter from Aunt Mattie's cow. The pigs provided ham, sausage, lard, and bacon. The chickens provided eggs as well as fried or baked chicken for Sunday dinners.

We also canned corn, chow-chow, pickles, tomatoes, and vegetable soup. Back then people ate from their gardens and animals. We had to plant and hoe gardens, get rid of bugs, then harvest everything. Digging potatoes at the end of summer was interesting. Uncle Guy plowed out the potatoes and Patty and I picked them up and put them in sacks or baskets.

Usually, we made a root cellar for storing cabbage, carrots, rutabagas, and onions. We just dug a good hole, placed the veggies in and covered them with lots of dirt.

Two funny things happened regarding the chickens and the rooster. Patty's worst enemy was the old rooster named Peter Arnell- Popeye-Guy. He didn't like Patty at all. One day when she went out, he wasn't in the chicken coop as usual. He came up to Patty and began "flogging" her. He had sharp nails on the backside of his legs and these nails hurt!

Well, on this one-day Patty grabbed the broom and took off after the rooster. Around and around the house they went.

The rooster finally gave out and just laid down. Patty took the broom and almost beat him to death! He finally got up and slowly walked back to the chicken coop. That's the last time he ever flogged Patty!

Another funny thing happened. It was up to Patty and me to kill a chicken every Saturday for Sunday's dinner. One time we laid the hen on the chop block and Patty took the axe and tried to chop its neck in two. (We hated this job, as we felt so sorry for the poor chicken.) The axe didn't quite cut all the way through the neck and that poor chicken jumped off the chop block and started running around with its head hanging down on its side! Neither of us have ever forgotten that poor chicken! Well, we caught it, finished the job, and got its head cut off, put it in the hot water, then plucked the feathers off (it stunk!). We then took a lighted piece of paper and burned the fine hairs off the body. Then we had to cut it up! Ooooooh!

THANKSGIVING AND HOG KILLING TIME

Every Thanksgiving while we lived with Aunt Maggie's was hog killing time. Patty and I wondered why the hog killing had to be done on a holiday, but looking back, I can see that it had to be a day when the men were off work.

Uncle Guy worked in a coal mine somewhere between Pax and Charleston, our Capitol City. It was known as the Kingston Mine. He wasn't much for hanging around the house and he wasn't very talkative. I wonder if I ever thanked him for providing for us for six years. Anyway, one of the men would shoot the hog and then they scraped the hair off the hog. It was a busy day, keeping the fire going under the big tub of water. The men had to put the hog in the water and then scrape all the hair off it. Then came the hard part- cutting up the animal! Various parts of the hog made diverse kinds of pork meat.

The women had to can the meat, make sausage, and do the cleanup work. Patty and I hated hog killing day. But the slabs of bacon they put in the smokehouse and the canned sausage were good breakfast foods and lasted all winter. Patty and I found out that we could blow up the bladder of the hog and use it for a balloon.

Living life in those days was quite different than the way people live today. We had no TV, no running water, no bathroom and only got a refrigerator during the last year we were there. The best I can figure we lived there from 1941 to 1946. I never knew where Paul and Gee Gee were living during those years. Paul showed up occasionally. He was only 13 when mother died. Gee Gee came sometime but not as often as Paul did. Paul loved to go to Aunt Hattie's as did Patty and me.

Aunt Hattie was such a cheerful person. She had a nicer house --a real living room with even a piano which she allowed us to try to learn to play. I learned a few things and it gave me a real desire to learn to play the piano which I did as I grew older. Aunt Hattie also had a bathroom, which we loved, with a pump in the basement which pumped water into the house. She had rows of kitchen cabinets and counters which was so different from Aunt Maggie's one little cabinet. Her house seemed so big compared to Aunt Maggie's house. Once when Patty and I walked from Aunt Maggie's to Aunt Hattie's in the summer during my first grade in school, I broke my right arm.

We were taking the long way walking around the road from Pax to Packs Branch and Mount Hope. Aunt Hattie lived on Packs Branch Road. If we took the shortcut, we went up the railroad track, past the old swimming hole through the woods, over the Creek via a log across the Creek like a bridge and then through a field on to Aunt Hattie's. But we were walking up the road when a horse in that unfenced field was running, frolicking, and coming straight toward us!

We were so scared that we climbed up a nearby tree. The horse turned around and went back, but I had a bad accident. I happened to step on a dead limb, fell out of the tree and wouldn't you know -- I landed on that flat rock! It addled my brain and when I got up, I had a pain in my back and especially in my right arm. It hurt so badly that I cried.

I don't remember whether we told Aunt Hattie about the incident, but I sure do remember my arm hurting badly and it was beginning to swell as we walked back to Aunt Maggie's. I remember a car going by with their radio on. The song "What A Friend We Have in Jesus" was playing and I thought God was trying to comfort me with those words. Now I know He was because even as a child I knew Jesus walks with us throughout our life's journey. Anyway, my arm hurt all night and I couldn't sleep. Finally, one or two days later, Aunt Maggie sent Patty and me down to Doctor Alfred Hunter's office in town. When we walked in, he took one look at me and said, "How did you break your arm?" It was black, blue, and swollen. He said, "You'll have to go to Oak Hill Hospital and let them fix it."

I remember Aunt Hattie got someone to drive us the fifteen miles to the city of Oak Hill where a nice doctor named Dr. Thompson, set my arm, and put a cast on it. That was the summer of 1941 when I was six years old. Patty was such a comfort to me. Uncle Guy's United Mine Workers insurance paid for the doctors. Anyway, it was a big disappointment, when in the first grade I was one of the top-ranking students but didn't pass because of a hateful teacher who wouldn't pass me because I couldn't write very well because I had to write with my left hand.

Charles Nelson Williams was the highest ranking first-grader, and I was right up there with him, but I got no recognition. All my life I loved learning and always made high grades clear through high school and much later through college.

Larry Tyree, the mayor's son, was in my grade. He always did well too. Faye Billups always did well. I will never forget most of my classmates from first grade through high school and some in college. Faye Billups was my best friend in grade school. Every year until just the last few years, Pax had a big reunion. Everybody came back from many states and Pax in their surrounding areas. There was a grade school and brick high school. I used to play softball during recess and Patty, being in the brick building, danced during lunch recess. That's where she learned to dance. Patty always did well in school. I can remember to this day her learning to sing her part in a school play.

KIDNAPPED

One Sunday evening, we went to church as usual. Herbert and Wilma, and Yvonne were outside the church waiting on us. Yvonne's husband Jerry was in the Navy currently. After church was over, we ran to them, they told us to get into the car and said we were going to their house! We were so excited! I wondered what Aunt Maggie would think when we didn't come home from church. Would she be worried or upset at us? We stayed the night, and I knew she would be worried.

The next day, one of Daddy's older sisters, Aunt Hattie (Harriet Brunk Tyree, born 1886), had someone drive her over to Garten to Wilma's house. When she arrived, Patty and I ran to the toilet to hide. Aunt Hattie told everybody that Aunt Maggie suffered a heart attack because of what we had done. Patty said," I'm not going back there."

I said," We must go back if we are the reason she had a heart attack."

I finally talked Patty into going back into Wilma and Herbert's house to face the music. It wasn't pleasant. We told Aunt Hattie we were sorry we caused Aunt Maggie to have that heart attack. She said, "The only way you can make it better is for you to let us take you back there."

So that is what happened. We dreaded telling Wilma goodbye and leaving. We loved it there but of course we hadn't brought any clothes or anything with us. When we got back home to Aunt Maggie's house, she seemed OK to us. I guess the shock of it all had unnerved her. I think Doctor Hunter had come up to see her. She was "smoking her powders."

I'll explain here about Aunt Maggie's powders. Years ago, some man who was selling herbs and other things told her he had an old Indian cure for asthma. She would take the powders out of the little can and spread them on top of the can on the lid. Then she would strike a match to make them burn. She would cup her hands around the smoke coming from the lid and inhale it. It would usually quiet an asthma attack quickly. We were all well acquainted with this way of dealing with her asthma. She had to "smoke her powders" several times a day. It did seem to help her.

We apologized again for upsetting her. I wondered if Yvonne and Wilma had contacted Daddy somehow about taking us to live with them. Aunt Maggie accused Yvonne and Wilma of plotting against her because she said now that we were old enough to help her with the work around there, they wanted us now. That wasn't the reasoning behind it at all though.

Yvonne, Wilma, and Herbert had talked with the mayor of Pax, Frank Tyree and he said he thought the best thing for us two girls was to live with our older sisters. He had heard from others in Pax that Aunt Maggie was so hard on us. He said everyone there in Pax knew what a hard life we lived at that house.

We had a little bit of time to play, but not very much. By the time we did all the work at the house, the yard, the garden, feeding the animals and doing our schoolwork, there was truly little time to just be kids. There was one thing that we really enjoyed. We had a darling cat named "Midnight." She was black and loved to be petted.

Shortly after the "kidnapping event," Daddy came home. We were so excited to see him. But that night, Uncle Guy and Daddy had their fight. I awoke to loud, angry voices. Daddy and Uncle Guy were standing in front of the fireplace arguing. One of them picked up a large clock sitting on the mantle and was starting to hit the other one on the head with that heavy clock. Uncle Guy picked up the clock and was going to strike Daddy. I screamed and they stopped and stood still. All the arguing and screaming woke Patty up.

The argument ended and a day or two later Patty and I got our things together to leave. I don't know why, but I surmised that Uncle Guy was tired of supporting us two little girls and Daddy who probably didn't help any. I'll never know, but that is what I think. Since Daddy only came in occasionally, Uncle Guy felt like Daddy was only visiting and not planning to help support his own children.

All I really know is Daddy and Patty took me to the train

station at PAX and sent me on my way to Yvonne and Jerry's house in Maben. I was 10 or 11 years old, scared, and lonely, wondering what was truly going on.

Jerry Stover, Yvonne's husband, came to get me when we got to Maben. Jerry was an electrician at the Maben mine. Yvonne later told me that he cried when he saw the condition, I was living in. I had on a pair of old women's high heeled shoes and looked like a Raggedy Ann. He told Yvonne to take me to Mullins in the next town and buy me some new clothes and shoes. So, I went from Cinderella one day to a Princess the next day. I'll never forget those beautiful clothes. I even had a beautiful blue plaid coat and cap. Life began anew for me on that special day.

To this day I don't know how Patty got to our sister Wilma's house in Garten in Fayette County near Fayetteville WV. Anyway, it turned out to be the best thing that had happened to us since Mother died.

WORLD WAR II (1941-1945)

GEORGE GRIFFITH BRUNK (GEE GEE)

Every day we turned on the radio to get the news about the war. We heard how the Japanese bombed one of our cities, Pearl Harbor in Hawaii on December 7th, 1941. Aunt Maggie always made sure we got the news by the CBS Radio news announcer named Peter Arnell. As time moved on, we heard about the maneuvers of the Allied Forces, about Adolph Hitler's terrible army as they moved with hopes of conquering the entire world. We didn't hear at that time about all the horrible atrocities done to the Jewish people. But as the days and years rolled on, we began to hear about the concentration camps.

We loved President Roosevelt. I loved hearing him talk and sometimes his wife, First Lady Eleanor. We did pray a lot about the war asking God to keep our fighting men safe, many of them died defending our nation.

I didn't know at that time that our brother Gee Gee had joined the army. I didn't know until much later that he was in the Battle of the Bulge, a terrible battle in or near the Black Forest in Germany. If I remember right, he never talked about the war to us. Anything about his time in the war I owe mostly to Patty and a chapter in her book she published several years ago, a delightful book called "Patty's Promise."

We loved President Roosevelt. I loved hearing him talk and sometimes his wife, First Lady Eleanor. We did pray a lot about the war asking God to keep our fighting men safe, many of them died defending our nation.

I didn't know at that time that our brother Gee Gee had joined the army. I didn't know until much later that he was in the Battle of the Bulge, a terrible battle in or near the Black Forest in Germany. If I remember right, he never talked about the war to us. Anything about his time in the war I owe mostly to Patty and a chapter in her book she published several years ago, a good book called "Patty's Promise."

A GREAT DAY FOR AILENE - 1946

Finding Jesus as Her Savior

One Sunday evening in March when I was 11 years old, we had a revival at our church, the Church of Christ in the town of Pax, West Virginia. It was a two-week revival. Patty and I were living with Aunt Maggie. We went to all the church services. We only had to walk on the "Red Dog" Road down our hill and about one thousand yards on down into the village. The church was constructed on a large hill which was entirely rock.

I always thought about the words Jesus used about men building their home on solid rock instead of shifting sand. That night the evangelist, Brother Duane Cooke, preached a good sermon about salvation and living a life that pleased our Heavenly Father. I realized I was a sinner, and I went forward as the congregation was singing the song entitled, "Oh Why Not Tonight."

Something really spoke to my heart, and I know it was truly the Holy Spirit. So, I left our pew and went to the front where evangelist and Deacon Ray Thompson and Clint Lively shook my hand and talked with me about accepting the gift of Jesus' blood to wipe away my sins. I agreed with them and soon the service ended.

It was the practice of the Church of Christ and all Christian churches that baptism should follow the act of salvation immediately. Since this was a small church, it had no baptismal.

So, the church members always went down to Paint Creek which was not too far from the church. The baptismal pool was a wide curve in the Creek below the Virginian Railroad where the things that cars hauled were unloaded and where passengers got on and off the passenger cars.

It was March and ice rimmed the edges of Paint Creek. It was extremely cold. I don't remember anyone putting any extra clothing on me before or after the baptism. I do remember being cold. But someone in the crowd told me they did not know of anyone having ever gotten sick because they were baptized in freezing water or chilly weather.

Aunt Maggie was pleased when we got home, and we told her all about the baptism. I know I was glad to get out of the wet clothes. I think someone in the crowd wrapped a big towel or blanket around me as I exited the Creek. I took my salvation seriously. I started reading my Bible every day.

The church only used the New Testament for Sunday school. I don't know if they used the Old Testament or not. But many of the scriptures I now know, I learned in that church. We were taught to memorize scriptures and we often had Bible quizzes which we loved. I remember one time we were having a spelling quiz of Bible names and they gave me the word "zurubabel" and I spelled it correctly. Strange that I would remember things like that.

One summer, we had a singing school led by a man who traveled from church-to-church teaching music. His name was O.O.Kidd. Of course, Patty and I wanted to go since we both loved music and Daddy had taught us how to sing the three parts of harmony: soprano, alto and tenor.

It cost a significant amount of money to attend that school, but we were so happy when Ray Thompson and Clint Lively told us they were going to pay for us to attend. We were so grateful and happy. For two weeks we learned choir songs, congregation songs and children's songs. Two children's song that I distinctly remember were a song in one of our song books titled "Swinging Beneath" the "Old Apple Tree" and one titled "The Cat Came Back." I remember the lyrics and the melody to this day.

One thing I remember grappling with was going to the movies. Our sister Wilma's boyfriend, Herbert Turner, ran the projector at the local movie theater. Mr. Skaggs owned the theater, and it was next to Canterbury's grocery store where we shopped. Herbert either talked Mr. Skaggs into letting us see movies every so often for free or else Herbert paid our fare. We really did enjoy the movie stars like Roy Rogers, Dale Evans, Gene Autry, and others. I can't remember but they were all clean movies. We never saw one with violence, sexual exploits, or murder except for shooting in the westerns.

One night on the way up the hill to Aunt Maggie's, I told Patty that I wondered if I was doing right by going to the movies. Patty said she didn't think we were doing wrong because it was all clean and Herbert wouldn't let us do it if it was wrong. So, I quit worrying about it.

We did enjoy church and had a big laugh one day when one of the main choir members on a Sunday morning was singing. She had her mouth wide open, and a fly flew into her mouth, and she choked and quit singing. I remember her name was Mrs. Lafferty. We all enjoyed a good laugh about that, except Mrs. Lafferty.

One beautiful Sunday during that summer, Clint Lively brought his big truck to the church. It was the day of the church picnic. The men put church pews in the back of the truck and all the people climbed in for a fun day. We took off for Grandview State Park and the 4-H Lake at Beaver Dam. They had several picnic tables in a big building with an outdoor shelter where some young people were dancing. They had music coming from a big jukebox.

You could buy ice cream and pop at the shelter building. Someone paid for boat rentals, and we got to go boat riding and swimming or wading in the water. There was lots of tasty food made by the ladies of the church. Anne Hattie took some sandwiches made of peanut butter and bananas which we had never eaten before. We went back to the church before dark, but we had such a wonderful day. The church people

were often doing good things for the two little "orphan girls."
Our Mother and Daddy had taken us to a Presbyterian
Church at Cunard close to Brooklyn. We had a good start in
life since Mother and Daddy had taken us to church and then
at Aunt Maggie's we went to the Church of Christ. I give
credit to Ray Thompson and Clint Lively for teaching us so
many scriptures which I can still quote to this day. It was truly
a Christian foundation.

I never remember Aunt Maggie or Uncle Guy going to
church while we lived there. Grandma couldn't go, of course,
and really neither could Aunt Maggie. She never could walk
far because of her asthma. Occasionally, her asthma got so
bad we had to go get Dr. Hunter to come and give her a shot.
Of course, Patty and I had to go get the doctor because we
didn't have a phone.

We used to go get the mail at the post office and go to
Canterbury's store to get a few groceries. Occasionally on
a Sunday, company would come. I especially liked it when
Thelma and Mack Meador visited. They always brought us
clothing which their daughter Frances Anne didn't need
anymore. She always had nice clothes. Mack would often give
us a little money so we could go to the store and get candy
and pop.

Thelma was the daughter of Aunt Fannie, who lived in
Beckley on North Pike Street. Thelma was a teacher and
she taught Arnold Deck, who would later be my husband.
Their two daughters Ruth and Frances Anne became teachers

and later they taught both of my sons, Mark, and Kevin, at Mabscott Elementary School in Beckley.

IT'S A WONDERFUL LIFE - 1946

Yvonne and Jerry lived at Maben near Mullins in Wyoming County. Jerry was an electrician at the mines in Maben in Wyoming County. He had a respectable job. We lived in a four-room company house. The Coal Company owners provided housing (for a fee) and a company store. Prices were higher at the company store but for those who didn't own a car, they had to buy their necessities there. The store was like a department store where you could buy clothing, household items, anything

JERRY AND YVONNE STOVER WITH CHILDREN
RONALD, DIANA AND LINDA

you needed. They took the cost of rent and your bill at the store out of the man's paycheck. This was customary practice at Coal Companies in those days.

Yvonne and Jerry had a bedroom with a crib for Diana who was about 16 months old. She was so cute. Ronald was five years old, and I slept in his room. Yvonne wanted it pretty for me, so she put glittering stars on the ceiling. They were beautiful! Now today I have shiny stars on my bedroom ceiling. Life was so different there. I felt like I really belonged to the family. I was 11 years old when I went there to live. I felt like this was really my home. I enrolled in the 6th grade at Maben Grade School and made the highest grades.

My close friends where Sarah Lou Jenks and her brother Van D. Jenks, who was the class clown. Other good friends were David McCoy who let me ride his bike. David ran for a legislative office this year, but he was now using his original name before he was adopted. He now goes by his real name David "Bugs" Stover. Ruth McGrady was another good friend. Phyllis and Dewey Houck were special friends. Phyllis became a nurse and I later read in the paper that she died young; I think as the result of a car wreck. Other close friends were Betty and Carolene Meadows who lived next door.

Two sisters Radene and Yvonne Vaught and I formed a girls' trio and sang at the local churches. Another close friend was Fay French whose last name now is Ball and lives in Mullens, WV.

The principal, Mr. Ted Clay, would let us bring our younger

siblings to school on certain days. Mr. Clay said Ronald was very smart.

I remember some of the pretty clothes and shoes Yvonne and Jerry bought me. There was a beautiful blue checked coat and cap and I sure felt like a queen, in my beautiful new clothes. By this time Jerry and Yvonne had bought a beautiful blue DeSoto car. Yvonne learned to drive. Wilma and Herbert had a car and almost every weekend we drove to Wilma and Herbert's house at Garten, or they drove to our house, and we often played cards, mostly Canasta.

On the way to Yvonne and Jerry's I was so excited! It was the first time I had ridden a train. I'd like that, but I got really nervous when we went over a trestle and there were several of those. Jerry came to meet me when we got to Maben. It had originally been a company that did lumbering and later became a coal camp.

When Jerry met me, I was so happy. Later, Yvonne told me he cried when he told her how I looked when I arrived there. He said I had on a pair of old ladies' high heel shoes, and I really looked like a poor orphan. He told Yvonne to take me to Mullens and buy me clothes. So, she did. I felt like a queen in my new clothes. I had new underclothes, school clothes, shoes and socks like the other girls wore. No more long black stockings and feed sack dresses! Looking back, Aunt Maggie did her best to clothe us. She made all our clothes on her old Singer sewing machine. But I turned from Cinderella to a Princess overnight.

After Jerry bought the blue DeSoto car, we took a trip to Outer Banks, NC and it was wonderful! Life was such a different kind of life now. Life was fun. Fortunately, I was well accepted at school by the students and staff. Yvonne had another darling baby girl named Linda Kay, who was born at home at Maben.

Boy, was life different now from the previous years. We felt loved and wanted. But I guess we had learned much about work ethics while at Aunt Maggie's. Patty and I helped Yvonne and Wilma with the housework and loved to babysit when the adults went somewhere. Herbert and Wilma had two little girls, cute as could be, named Lana Joy and Brenda Carol.

Patty went to junior high and high school at Fayetteville, WV in Fayette County. That's where Patty graduated from high school. She got a job at the Garten Company Store, and she had several close friends there. One friend of hers I remember was Betty Jo Epperly. Patty graduated from Fayetteville high school in 1952.

Shortly after graduation, Herbert went to Jackson, Michigan and got an excellent job at Goodyear in 1952. He worked there many years and retired years later and he and Wilma moved to the Villages in Florida. While in Michigan, Wilma had gone to college. Wilma had taken the test and became a licensed cosmetologist. She had her own beauty salon which Herbert built for her in their basement in Michigan. After moving to Florida, she worked at another beauty salon.

One real tragedy took place in their family while living in

Michigan: Brenda contracted encephalitis and while in the hospital she went to her eternal heavenly home. She was only days shy of her 13th birthday. We have missed her all these years, but we will see her again. She gave her life to Jesus as a child. She took her Salvation seriously. Brenda Carol Turner was beloved by everyone in the family.

I had a wonderful life at Yvonne and Jerry's,. Diana (age 16 months when I went there) and Ronald became my sister and brother. When we lived at Iroquois in Wyoming County, I went to Mullens High School. I was a top student. I joined the Schubert Choir, and we sang at other school graduations. While in high school, I had a boyfriend named Joe Robertson. He was so nice, and we spent time together at noon time. He was particularly good looking and a fine person. Unfortunately, he recently passed away.

While at Iroquois I got sick. Yvonne took me to many doctors. No one knew what was wrong. My side hurt and I had no energy. Finally, a doctor sent me to Dr. Snyder in Bluefield. I was in St. Luke's hospital for weeks. I entered the hospital November 3rd and I got out for Christmas. They said I had a bad case of hepatitis. I finished the first nine weeks of my junior year and had to miss all the rest of the school year. But I was in the hospital quite a bit that year.

During this time, I met Sterling Stewart, who was in the Air Force and visiting his sister who lived next door. He was from Pikeville, KY, came to see me at the hospital and we became close. He asked me to marry him. His sister, Katherine Brehm, asked me to go to Pikeville to visit their mother. So Sterling, Katherine, and I went. He had a nice family. I said I would marry Sterling, but he wasn't a Christian, so I wasn't sure it was the right thing to do. He would come and sit with me, and we would listen to records. He joined the Air Force, and he was stationed in Arizona.

SIDNEY AND AILENE AT
HER HIGH SCHOOL GRADUATION

Meanwhile Daddy had surgery in Wilmington, Delaware for brain cancer. He was able to come to my graduation in May 1955. He used a cane and I started giving him physical therapy. Yvonne was bedfast due to her 4th pregnancy. October 17th, 1955, she gave birth to her fourth child, Deborah Lynn.

I called Sterling and told him about a man I met named Arnold

Deck and that I fell in love with him. Sterling was so upset he flew home and begged me to change my mind. But I couldn't. I knew God meant for Arnold and me to spend our lives together. Sterling gave up. Meanwhile he had become a Christian. I was so happy about that.

In the summer of 1955 Arnold proposed to me and I felt it was God's will that we spend our lives together. He was such a good man and good Christian. So, between helping Yvonne with baby Debbie and taking care of Daddy, I managed to spend time with Arnold.

My illness had lasted a year and I had missed much of my junior year. Jerry, Yvonne, and family bought a home in Crab Orchard, WV where Arnold was born. I went to the big school called Woodrow Wilson High School when I graduated with high grades in May 1955.

While living at Iroquois, Yvonne, her family, and I went to a wonderful church, First Church of God in Mullens. We had several good friends there. After this chapter there's a short chapter about the time Jesus came to our house in Iroquois the night before we moved to Crab Orchard. The most exciting time of my life and I wanted a whole chapter about it. Meanwhile Daddy became worse, and he went to his heavenly home shortly after Arnold and I were married.

Arnold and I had a lovely wedding on Thanksgiving Day, November 24th, 1955. Velva was my Maid of Honor. Patty wasn't sure she could come but she did get to come. We had a lovely honeymoon at Renfro Valley, KY. Then we moved into the house Arnold and his dad Ezra had built after we had lived in their upstairs a little while.

Because I had only completed the first nine weeks of my junior year at Mullens High School, I had to start in my junior year at Beckley WV at Woodrow Wilson High School. When I graduated in May of 1955, I was 19 years old. Arnold was four years older than me. Due to Yvonne being bedfast in 1955, Aunt Hattie allowed us to bring Daddy down to her house at Packs Branch and I would go down there and spend the week taking care of Daddy. Arnold always took me there on Sunday evening and bring me back on Friday evening, even before we married. One weekend Arnold's mother, Thelma Deck, asked me to spend the weekend at her house because I looked so tired. She was so good to me, and I really rested.

Daddy was bedfast while at Aunt Hattie's. He only wanted me to bring him his cocoa which he dearly loved. We were able to talk about life and death. He had gone to church off and on for years, but I knew about the 15 years after mother died and he had become an alcoholic, I guess. So, I talked to him about his eternal soul and how he needed to make things right with his heavenly Father.

So, one day he prayed the Sinner Prayer and assured me everything was right between him and God. I called Gee Gee in Delaware and told him Daddy's health was critical. Gee Gee said he would come and get him. He came as he said he would. Arnold took Gee Gee, Daddy, and me to Charleston to the airport.

The last time I saw Daddy alive was when he was in a wheelchair. Gee Gee and airport personnel put him on the plane. Daddy died on December 14th, 1955 – fifteen years after Mother had died. She had died on Friday the 13th of December 1940.

Daddy died in Delaware and all the family came to Aunt Hattie's. for the wake, and I have a family picture of all of us out in Aunt Hattie's yard. I had contacted the minister who had baptized me in the creek near the Church of Christ and he so graciously held the funeral. The wake was well attended. Daddy was buried in the Pax Community Cemetery where my

WAKE AT AUNT HATTIE'S FOR SIDNEY BRUNK. PAUL AND PHYLLIS BRUNK, HERBERT AND WILMA , BRENDA TURNER, PATTY BRUNK AND BOYFRIEND ROY

brother Paul and his wife Joan were also buried.

I am inserting a lovely poem Paul's wife Joan wrote after she became a Christian. She and I became really close as well as Paul and their children. She had already had two daughters, Linda, and Mary, before she and Paul met. Their children are Lorraine Cobol, Paul Sidney Brunk, Jr., Paula Aileen Boan, Joy Weikle and Cynthia, Cindy McGhee. I still have letters Paul and Joan wrote Arnold and me after we went to Delaware and led him to the Lord when Paul almost committed suicide. Arnold bought $100 worth of groceries and clothes for the family and since it was Thanksgiving, nearly Christmas, Arnold bought tickets for the whole family to come to our house for Christmas on the train. That led them to want to move to West Virginia.

Patty and Yvonne each gave Paul $1,000 for a down payment on a fire damaged house which Yvonne, Jerry, Arnold and I, and some Christian friends, Chuck, and Caren Norris, worked on to make it livable for them to move into when they moved to West Virginia. They made it into a beautiful home.

A PRAYER OF THANKS - BY JOAN BRUNK (1976)

(JOAN BRUNK WAS THE WIFE OF AILENE'S BROTHER PAUL BRUNK)

Oh, Father of Mine, did I thank you today,
For all that You've given me, along life's way.

Did I thank you just now, for my Savior above?
To know that I've been, "washed in His blood".

Did I thank you, Dear Father, for hearing my prayers,
And comforting my heart, when trouble is near?

Did I tell you today, "I Love You So"?
And long to be with you wherever you go.

I know, Dear Father, in heaven above,
A new home awaits me, full of much love,

How can I thank you, for all that you have given,
Living my life, on this earthly prison.

But then I know you have a plan for me,
So mold my life, as you would want it to be.

Thank you, Dear Father, for all of your love,
And thank you, Dear Father for my savior above.

TERROR ON A THIRTEENTH HALLOWEEN - OCT 1947

I wrote this novelette for a college creative writing project

It was a perfect autumn night. The air was crisp and clean smelling. Jack Front had visited the scraggly, leftover sand briars and ragweed that the bush-hog had missed. The grass was so frosty that it was scrunchy underneath our feet.

The full moon peeped through the tall pines. The pond had a razor-thin coat of ice on its edges. I was a scrawny twelve-year-old scaredy cat accompanied by my fourteen-year-old self-appointed hero of a brother, Paul.

Everyone loves a clown, and my brother fit the bill. You could just see the mischief sticking out of him, and the way he sauntered down the path, you would think he owned the world. I felt secure with him beside me. Anyway, I surely was glad that I wasn't alone because tonight was Halloween.

We had attended a masquerade party at our neighbor's just over the ridge about a mile from home. It was a great party with lots of games, prizes, food, and neat costumes. We had enjoyed our hostess' ghost stories immensely. "She is a great storyteller," I said as we happily walked down the winding path which became darker and scarier with each step. The scraggly pines made eerie looking shadows that were reaching out to get me, but I put on my brave, big-girl act and kept right on walking.

"Yeah," Paul said. "But they weren't all made up stories. The one about old man Gillenwater is true."

"Naw," I said. "It couldn't be."

"Oh, but Daddy told me that same story several years ago," Paul replied. "Exactly the way Mrs. Shoemaker told it tonight. It really did happen! On Halloween night."

"Old man Gillenwater was walking down this very path on a dark Halloween night when he was suddenly lifted high into the air. He didn't know what had happened, but later found out that he had stepped into a snare, an animal trap, which caught his foot, snapped him high above the tree and jerked him back and left him hanging there upside down."

"Luckily, Dad came along a couple of hours later and got him down.

He would have died there hanging by one foot, upside down in the cold darkness. No one ever knew if it was deliberate or an accident."

"Dad said that every thirteenth year, on Halloween night, at midnight, weird things happen. You know, every thirteen years something else weird-like does happen. It so happens that Mr. Gillenwater's accident occurred twenty-six years ago today at midnight."

"What time is it?" I asked shakily.

"Fifteen 'til twelve," Paul replied.

A shiver started at the base of my skull, shimmied down my spine, ran straight down my right leg and out my big toe. That's what happens to me when I am really frightened.
"Well, I am not afraid," I bragged. And we've only got about half-a-mile to go." I sure hoped we could get home by midnight! I found myself stretching my legs, trying to cover as much ground as possible. Then it happened!

I screamed as I felt myself falling into an unfamiliar hole. The earth opened to swallow me! My fingers clutched at rocks and dug into the dirt along the sides of the hole, and the dry, musty odor of the soil filled my nostrils. It was so woodsy and pungent I could taste it. "Ugh-a-doo-ker-choo," I half sneezed and coughed. I screamed and clawed at the earth, which was trying to claim my body. "Help!" I yelled.

Paul reached down toward me. Our fingers touched but couldn't quite meet. "Jump!" he shouted, and I will grab you!" I was so shaky I didn't know if I could jump. About that time, I heard the awfullest sound I had ever heard in my life. It was indescribable. A terrible screeching sound. "Ahh-rick-a-roo-

196 | Lily Ailene Deck

chi-ruii" it went. "Ahh-rick-a-roo-chi-ruii"

It sounded like a bunch of giant fingernails scratching on a giant chalk board, or worse. It scared me so badly that with one big hop, I was out of the hole.

"What was that?" I whispered, too afraid to speak aloud.

"Aw, just some old screech owls," Paul said. "Didn't you ever hear screech owls before?"

"No," I replied. Hoot owls yes, but not screech owls. Awfullest sound I ever heard! Boy that fall and these screech owls about scared me to death. Let's get out of here!"
The moon, which had been playing peek-a-boo behind thick, dark clouds, now chose to play hide and go seek. It hid itself so well that not a shred of light could peek through.

Was it just that I was scared, or was it that much colder? The icy fingers of the frosty night air reached around my throat, slipped down the back of my neck and began to pluck the taut, yellow strings of my spinal cord like those of a banjo strung too tightly. It chilled me to my bone marrow. Never had I been this cold!

The thought of that old man Gillenwater hanging upside down in the cold darkness began to nag at me. What if something happened before we reached home? I carefully set each foot down as if I could avoid a trap or a snare.

Suddenly, I felt my bare left footstep into something cold and squishy. "Oh my," I hollered. "A doggone cow pie!"

Paul, the clown prince, doubled over with laughter. He looked so funny standing there all bowed over holding his sides laughing. He was so comical looking in his hobo outfit, that I began to laugh with him.

We had gone to the party as a hobo and hobo-ette. He had on a too-large pair of bibbed overalls with one strap missing and a red checkered shirt with a bunch of holes in it and frayed sleeves. One sleeve hung down to his fingertips: the other to his elbow. The crazy quilt patterned patches sewn on the overalls were red, yellow, pink, and some polka-dotted purple and green ones. Even with no moonlight they stuck out like a holey diaper on a baby's bottom. He topped it all off with an old straw hat minus the brim, with long straws sticking out all over, porcupine fashion. He carried an old fishing pole with a red, white, and black stuffed bandana swinging jauntily at the end. It was filled with candies from the party. He was also barefooted.

My hobo-ette costume, a little less imposing, was like his, except I had on an old holey and similarly patched denim skirt and a ragged pukey-purple and pink bandana pushing back my light brown hair. I carried an old raggedy, yellow cloth handbag, also full of goodies. I was also barefooted.

That old cow manure squished up through my toes and did it stink! I walked over to a spot where the grass was higher and began scooting my foot through the tall weeds trying desperately to rid my foot of the foul-smelling greenish, ghoulish looking goo.

Suddenly, I was lifted into the air! My heart began to thump hard enough to jump out of my throat. My blood turned to ice water. I screamed, "What is happening?" I didn't know. All I knew was I was being carried away!

Through the darkness, Paul could see nothing more than a little hobo-ette flying, unlike the girl of the flying trapeze, with much less than the greatest of ease.

And me? All I knew was that something was underneath me, pouncing and pounding, hooves beating on the hardened path. The backbone of the creature upon which I tremblingly hunched was hard and sharp and it dug into my behind. It felt like I was riding on a huge bone. I was flying with the speed of a demon. Where was this demon creature headed? Never in my short lifetime had I experienced anything like this!

My fingers dug into some stiff hair-like substance. I got a deadbolt finger hold and dug in even deeper. I wrapped my legs around the neck of I know not what, bowed my body low and hung on for dear life. I had my legs locked around that neck so tightly, that the muscles of my legs felt totally and permanently locked. In front of me, I could see long, slender spiney-looking tenacles stretched out and upwards. There was a dozen of those things out there! What was this thing plunging over the earth with an ungodly speed? I thought again about Mr. Gillenwater and about the thirteenth Halloween. And I wondered what time it was. Would I die a premature death on Halloween?

The last glimpse I had of Paul, he was running after us hollering, "WHOA! STOP! Come back here you varmint!" But alas, now he was out of sight. And I was plunging into the thick darkness, farther and farther from Paul and from sanity. My legs were aching so badly from that locked-in position. My arms felt like a terrific toothache. The wind whipped my bandana off and the roar of it flapped my ears like a crow's wings. That awful sound of the snorting creature was sickening. Who or what was this demon that carried me to heaven knows where?

Suddenly, the roar of the wind grew quieter in my ears. We came to a barrier and the creature tried to jump. I felt it rise higher and I dug in deeper with my aching finger grip. Whump! Thud! We fell into a heap upon the frosty ground. I lay there numb and feeling dead. About that time, the moon peeked out from hiding. I saw long, slender, brown hair covered legs and hooves thrashing around my own slender legs. We were all in one big heap. This thingamajig was trying to get up. Would it gobble me up or what? It struggled to its feet and stood up. I arose to a sitting position to get a better look at my tormentor.

Why, it was a beautiful buck deer! It had a huge twelve-point rack on its stately head. With tender, sorrowful looking eyes, he looked at me as if to apologize. Poor thing! I must have scared him as much as he had scared me.

A fleeting glance at me and he was gone, dashing easily over the fence, down the hill, to be lost from view in the stand of dark shadowy pines. I picked myself up and, rubbing my aching muscles, I started limping over the cold-hard-frozen ground. My feet were freezing so I started a kind of skip and hop motion to keep them off the ground even if for just a little while. Not knowing if I was headed in the right direction or not, I plodded on. My whole body hurt. I was trembling and felt numb from fright and the coldness.

Ahead I saw a familiar landmark and knew I wasn't far from home. Years ago, lightning had struck a huge tree and burned out all but the outer hull. The inside had proved to be a safe haven during storms for many a traveler over the path. Its several long straggly branches, way up high, cast dark sinister looking shadows as they reached out like the long skinny arms of an over-sized witch. Inside the tree, the space could accommodate several people. Many times, when we kids played hide and seek, we used the hollow tree. I longed for the soft feel of the rotten bark covering the floor of the tree. I limped into it and fell to the floor to rest my weary bones.

Alas, I wasn't alone. In the darkness, I couldn't see but could feel a presence. "Oh no! What now," I thought. Remaining as quiet as possible, I hunkered down and back against the soft side of the tree, making myself as small as possible. Was it, or he, or she, as scared as I? Was the creature about to burst from holding its breath, as I was? I let out my breath as softly as I could, but it sounded loud like a hissing sound, probably because I was so scared.

Should I crawl out, sit still, run or scream? As if reading my thoughts, the other occupant gingerly reached out in my direction. A cold hand touched my face and I shuddered and then screamed. I grabbed that hand and flung it away from me. And then the fight was on. We fought like two wild cats. We slugged and banged, hit, and yelled. I ducked a blow and realized I was panting, and my breath felt cold on my nose. Suddenly, the moon came out from hiding and we froze, his hand in the air, mine ready for an uppercut. I looked into those familiar liquid-blue eyes and yelled, "Paul!"

"Ailene," he screamed. "What the...where? Oh, gosh," he sighed.
We fell to the ground and too tired to laugh or cry, wrapped our arms around each other. How could I have known it was him? Or he, me?

"What happened out there?" he almost yelled.

"Would you believe I walked right up on to the back of a big buck," I asked,

"No!"

"Well, it was some ride."

"How did you get away?" he asked.

"You know that old rail fence down at the far end of the field?

"Yeah."

"Well, he tried to jump it but didn't make it," I replied.

"We fell hard. He finally got his senses back, gave me the once-over and took off."

"Wow!" was his reply. "A big one, huh?"

"Yeah, a twelve-pointer. Boy, could he fly. At first, I didn't know what had happened. I thought of old Gillenwater. I thought I was a goner. I held on for dear life and when we fell, I think I must have been too stunned to know anything. I thought I was dead! Boy, this is one night I will never forget."

"And where were you, dear hero of mine?" I queried.

"Following you and that thing, yelling my head off, freezing my feet and wondering if I'd ever see you again. After you were out of sight, I decided to come here into our old tree and try to decide whether to go look for you or go get Dad."

"Well, my feet are ice, my legs are like dead logs, and I've just about shaken out of my skin and these hobo-ette clothes. But I think I can make it home."

"Good. Let's go "Paul said. But I won't let you out of my sight again. Hold on to my hand."
I wasn't about to let go.

"Paul, what time is it?

"Twenty minutes past midnight," he replied.

"Whoop-de-do!" I yelled. "We made it past midnight on the thirteenth Halloween, cheated death and we are almost home." The light in the frosted window of the front door beckoned me. What a welcome sight! The moon sailed on through the clouds. The screech owls started up that horrendous cacophony. I made it through the door and into Daddy's open arms. And passed out cold!

ARNOLD AND I GET MARRIED AND START OUR WONDERFUL FAMILY- NOV. 24, 1955

ARNOLD AND AILENE'S WEDDING

I read an article about Arnold Deck in the Beckley newspaper. He had volunteered to take a shipload of cattle to war torn Germany after he had finished two years of volunteer work for our church, the Church of the Brethren. While he was gone, my friend Velva Dolinger had invited me to go with her to the Church of the Brethren, where she attended. When she spent the weekend or a Saturday night with me, she went with me to my church, the Beckley First Church of God.

On the weekend that Arnold came back from Germany, I was visiting Velva and her church. I always went in the choir with Velva and Arnold was there singing tenor. I sang a solo that evening and Arnold told me much later that when I was singing, he said to himself, "I am going to marry that girl." We dated that year and in August Arnold proposed to me.

Velva and her friend Wade Cummings, and Arnold and I would go to one of the Beckley drive-ins, Pete, and Bob's. The other one was King Tuts. Velva and I had graduated from Woodrow Wilson high school in May 1955.

Our wedding was beautiful, and the service was held at the Brethren Church in Crab Orchard. Then we had a nice reception at Yvonne's house. Arnold and I went to Renfro Valley, Kentucky which is an old-fashioned community where the Sunday morning church broadcast originated, which we both had enjoyed for years. We took our trip using silver dollars that Arnold had been saving for many years. When God puts two people together in marriage, he means forever. We were married 63 years lacking one day. More about that later.

We lived in Arnold's parents upstairs until the people renting our house moved. We moved into the house that Arnold and his dad Ezra had built. Ezra was a well-known builder in the region. In fact, he built the Oak Grove Christian Church where our children and grandchildren now attend and where Arnold are buried in the church Cemetery and where I will someday be laid to rest. It is only located about 2 miles from our ranch.

Arnold and I were active in the Church of the Brethren. He was a Deacon and assistant choir director. He became the choir director when the director, Jim Stanley left. Later I became choir director. We taught Sunday School Classes and Arnold started a Boys Club which was always well attended. He took them on fishing and camping trips. We both were youth leaders at one time or another. We had about 275 members in the church at that time.

Life was wonderful. No one could tell all the marvelous things life holds for two people joined together by God. The happiest event in our lives at the time was the birth of our first son Mark Allen Deck, born February 8th, 1958, during a big snowstorm. He was born at the Beckley Hospital and was beautiful! He had blonde hair and blue eyes. He weighed eight pounds and ten and a half ounces and was 22-1/2 inches long. He was three weeks overdue. He slept all night, except for feeding time. God has been great to us.

Arnold had started working for C&P telephone company (now Verizon) about two months before we married. He worked there for 38 1/2 years, and retired in April, 1994. Our joy at Mark's birth was heightened by the birth of our second son, Kevin Ray Deck, two years, and nine months after Mark was born. He weighed 7 pounds, 15-1/2 ounces and was 21 1/2 inches long. He also had blonde hair and blue eyes and was born at the new Appalachian Regional Hospital. He was simply adorable!

MARK AND KEVIN DECK

Now we had two beautiful sons. I have never known two brothers to be as close as Mark and Kevin have been all their life. Of course, as children, they had their little spats. But as adults where one goes, you see the other one going. They work together on our ranch doing everything without arguing. When Mark is in his nice big garage and Kevin isn't at work, he's there working with Mark. When Kevin is in his nice big garage, if Mark can be there, he is there helping Kevin. Everywhere one of them went, they all went. Once they left for out of state to work, they both went, along with Jeff Campbell, who is like our son.

Mark and Kevin had their share of childhood illnesses and had their little spats as children do. Mark was more of a rambunctious nature, Kevin was thoughtful, quieter, and patient. They made friends easily and I've mentioned the names of their closest friends elsewhere in this book. I am so thankful that our sons have always been so close, like Patty and me. I guess the love and thoughtfulness that are displayed when children are growing up is what we could attribute that to. I only saw Kevin angry one time.

When they didn't have any work pressing them and needed a little rest, they would go up to our camp at Sherwood Lake in Greenbrier County. They would sit in front of the fire and go fishing or hunting.

Mark had a temper. At times he would bend forward and bang his head on the floor. One time Arnold went over to him and gently banged it on the floor for him. That was the last time he banged his head! I wanted desperately to bring our children up in the nurture and admonition of the Lord's scriptures. I bought them their little storybook Bibles and good books as they took an interest in learning. They both loved books. They played in Little League baseball for a while. They began to tire of it because they said it took all their time and they didn't have any time left to play at home. So, we allowed them to quit.

Drema and Kevin are close cousins. They were born nine hours apart on the 14th and 15th, of November in 1960. Once when Kevin and Drema were little, Drema followed the dog towards Grandaddy Deck's house out the lane. They often went there to get Aunt Emma's cookies. Well, Kevin followed, we thought, but he got lost (or we thought so.) Someone found Drema but we looked all over the place to find Kevin. We finally found him in his Momaw Deck's house behind the couch fast asleep.

Momaw and Popaw Deck lived in the big house just across the street on (Deck Lane) from our house. One day Kevin and Drema decided to get jewelry out of Janet's and my jewelry boxes and hide them like pirates do. Momaw had a place in her basement that was an unfinished small room where she kept the food she canned.

The walls in the room were not completed by the workers. There was just a dirt wall on one side. Kevin and Drema dug a hole in that wall and placed our jewelry in the hole and closed it up with dirt. Of course, the jewelry was inexpensive, but we hunted for it later anyway.

One day Popaw Deck decided to finish the walls of that cellar. By that time Drema and Kevin were back in school. They were later shocked when they found out the precious jewels had been sealed in the wall forever. And there they remain to this very day. Sometimes we have talked and laughed about the day the pirates took our jewelry.

I could write a whole book about Mark and Kevin growing up but that would be a long book. But I do want to talk about moving to a larger place with more acreage than we had before. They loved horses and had one named Sparky. We had to live on Momaw and Popaw's land.

One day Kevin and his close friend Eddie Hylton, who lived next door and another neighbor his age, named Phillip

Fondale, formed a club called the" Three Mighty Kings." They wanted to meet and do good things for the community. They would take their wagon and go along Old Eccles Road and pick up cans and trash. Someone saw them and admired their ambition. The following weekend their picture was in the paper and Jerry Cochran, owner of Beckley's only airport, called and told them that he was going to reward them by taking them for an airplane ride. They were five or six years old, and it was a real thrill for them. I'll never forget the Three Mighty Kings.

One time Mark's little dog got down on the highway and was hit by a car and killed. I saw Mark lying beside the road with his arms around his dog just crying his eyes out. I went to him and brought him and his dog home. As the boys grew up, they always had a dog. Every boy needs a dog. We had Cricket, Puff (number one) and Puff (number 2) and other dogs, two named Tippy and others.

Mark's friends while growing up were David Smith, Tim Murray, and others I can't remember. Tim's brother, Carl, was Kevin's friend and I talk about Greg Rodgers elsewhere in this book and about his sudden death.

Those Childhood Days

Today while standing at my kitchen sink,
I saw a sight which made me stop and think
Of how our days go floating swiftly by
As eagles grandly soaring through the sky.
My little boy, age six, was running merrily
Across the fields so full of childish glee.
A tear came to my eye, as thoughts I did employ,
That soon he will no longer be just a little boy.
For he will start to school this fall;
A few more years, he'll be so tall.
And not so very long from then
It seems he won't be mine at all.
Enjoy each childish moment, something seemed to say;
For soon these scenes, like sunshine quickly fade away.
Hold fast each childhood moment; watch the sunlight in each
face; For soon these little
childhood scenes, the hands of time erase.
Listen to their problems; Take some time for them.
And when they ask a question, it isn't just a whim.
They'd like to know some answers; They look to you with
pride.
To them, you're full of wisdom with such great strength inside.
I thought of how my little boy, now nine will soon grow into
Manhood- no longer will be mine. Oh yes, he'll always be my
son; But days of work and play
with him, they soon will all be done.
For children seem to have a way of quickly growing up

Like yellow scattered o'er the field-the short-lived buttercup.
Their childhood seems to vanish before its half begun.
So let them enjoy their childhood days, yes let them have their
fun.
Oh, let them run the fields in play
'Ere years so quickly slip away.
They have such few short years to enjoy
Their childhood as a little boy!

By: Ailene Deck, May 1967

THE NIGHT JESUS CAME TO OUR HOUSE

In 1954, my sister, Yvonne, and I, and eight or nine ladies from our church at South Mullins in Wyoming County had a most unusual experience which none of us could ever forget. Our church at that time was the first Church of God in South Mullens, West Virginia.

We had moved to a company house beside the Guyandotte River in Iroquois because Yvonne's husband, Jerry Stover, had found a better job with Semet-Solvay energy company at Trailee, South of Mullins. He was a well-respected electrician at that place of employment. He worked on the evening shift getting home around 2:00 AM.

We were all packed up and ready to move to Raleigh County to Crab Orchard where Yvonne and Jerry had bought a house. No longer would we live in the coal company houses! This house had plenty of room for their family of three children, me, and Yvonne and Jerry, with a nice yard, and enough room for a garden.

Several ladies of the church came to visit and to wish us well and tell us goodbye. They were dear, close friends. We had been talking and enjoying our time together when we heard the back door open. At that time, the living room filled with the most brilliant light I had ever seen! The strangest thing happened! All at one time, every person in the room fell to their knees. I felt hands go around my waist, lift me out of my seat and set me down on my knees! This happened to everyone in the room at the same time! Such a brilliance of light I or any of the others had ever experienced!

No one talked, except every few minutes someone would say glory to God, Hallelujah, Awesome God, Precious Jesus, and bless the Lord. All words were the words of praise to God, Jesus, and the Holy Spirit. Time stood still. There was no sense of time! Our minds were focused on the Father, Son, and the Holy Spirit.

I have no idea how long we stayed on our knees praising the Lord. Finally, one by one we started rising. We were filled with awe! Everyone's face glowed with a brilliant light or glow! We would make statements like, "We have never experienced anything like this!"

We had wallpaper with a leaf design. The leaves were highlighted with a brilliant light! Jerry came in around 2:00 AM and he knew something unusual was taking place. He went straight to his room and went to bed, which was unusual for him. Finally, we went outside, joined hands, and prayed and praised the Lord. It was the most wonderful experience I have ever had! You never forget things like this. What an experience when Jesus came to our house! Thank the Lord for this wonderful experience. God is so real! He loves us everyone so much! Praise His dear name!

UNCLE GUY'S QUESTIONABLE DEATH- 1959

In 1959. Uncle Guy was killed on the turnpike near the intersection of Interstate 64 and 77. That land earlier had been purchased by Uncle Guy and their house was on the top of a hill in Pax. Usually, the land on the hill behind the house became pastureland.

We heard that Uncle Guy's body was located beside the highway and there was a huge hole in the back of his head. No one had reported an accident on that road. Everyone in the family knew that Uncle Guy had a drinking problem, and he had several friends who drank and gambled with him at the local Pax Taverns.

The state always put a fence up on the property they bought for the highways. There was a huge chain link fence behind the house where the pastureland was located. The Pax people theorized that Uncle Guy was drunk, climbed over the fence and fell, rolling down the hill and ending up beside the highway. But the family didn't think that is what happened.

They didn't think anyone could climb that high chain link fence, drunk or sober. Aunt Hattie and Aunt Maggie believed many of his drinking and gambling friends lost some money to Uncle Guy and they killed him and placed his body there at the highway. I don't believe there was an investigation, so we will never know what really happened to him. He was never mean to us and supported us for six years while Daddy was wandering all over the country.

Also, when he died, Aunt Maggie and Grandma had no one to support them financially. Uncle Guy had his problems, but he had always been a good provider for his family. So, after his death, Aunt Maggie and Grandma had to rely on financial support from a government program they called, RELIEF.

Often in my life I have wondered what really did happen to Uncle Guy. All their family are buried in the Pax Community Cemetery. There are many of my family members buried in that cemetery, also. Grandma and Grandpa and a few of their children are buried there and it is the resting place where Aunt Hattie and some of her children are buried.

Aunt Maggie and Uncle Guy are buried there along with my own Daddy, my brother Paul, and his wife Joan. I go there on Memorial Day to celebrate their lives. Jerry Stover has some relatives buried in that same cemetery as well.

There was a stile on the fence between the cemetery and Aunt Rhoda Davis' land next to it. I used to love to go up and down that stile when I was a little girl. It's the only stile I ever saw. If you don't know what a stile is, it is a set of steps beside the fence that allows you to go up to a platform at the top and then cross over to another set of steps on the other side of the fence. It allows only people and not animals to climb over. This is how someone could get from one side of the fence to the other, without installing a gate.

A FATAL ACCIDENT -
JULY 23, 1973

One sweltering day in July 1973, the family had gone to Greenbrier County to visit Marion, Arnold's older sister, and her husband Clyde Tolbert at their cabin. We had gone there to enjoy their cabin and the summertime and to fish in their big pond.

Arnold's dad, Ezra Jefferson Deck, was a well-known and well-respected builder in the Beckley and surrounding area. In fact, he built a beautiful Oak Grove Christian Church, where our family goes to church.

Popaw, as we called him, had been up to Marion and Clyde's cabin and he came home to finish cutting hay on the hillside opposite their house. I guess maybe he was in a hurry to get it done and go back to the cabin which was 92 miles away. Kevin and Mark were in the field helping him in whatever way he needed such as getting him water.

Suddenly the tractor was tumbling down the hill and Popaw fell off. The tractor came tumbling after him. The tractor landed on top of Popaw! Mark and Kevin ran to his aid. Kevin took off running to Popaw and Momaw's house to have her call an ambulance.

Mark stayed right there with his beloved Popaw. Popaw said, "Mark, turn me over. I can't breathe lying here on my stomach and I'm burning up."

Mark said, "Popaw, I can't turn you over. If I do a broken bone might puncture a lung or your heart. I'll get something and fan you." Mark quickly broke off tree limbs and started fanning his Popaw. He kept saying to Popaw, "The ambulance and Momaw will be here soon."

The ambulance came and Mark told us when the medics turned Popaw over, Mark could hear the breath swoosh out of Popaw and his face turned gray. Mark said, "I knew right then that he had died." They pronounced him dead when they arrived at the hospital.

We never really knew what happened. One of the smaller wheels in front hit a hole or a dip in the contour of the land, or he had a heart attack and lost control. We never really found out what caused the accident and Arnold ended up inheriting that very same tractor.

We had always looked forward to going to Momaw and Popaw Deck's home for holidays such as Christmas. No one celebrated Christmas like they did, it was a wonderful family event. And Mama was such a great cook. She would have her families come for supper, and we would have all the family come to our houses to eat with us. Popaw especially loved fish dinners with fish the guys had caught. He loved them with hush puppies and slaw. The men in the family all loved to hunt and fish and the women learned to cook squirrel, rabbit, and fish.

We all miss those of our family who have made their journey to Jesus in that beautiful land! What a wondrous meeting there is going to be one day! And Jesus' death on the cross made it all possible. Part of our eternity will be in that city in the Sky and eventually we, with our new bodies, will live on this planet after God has cleansed it and made it like the Garden of Eden. At least, that is the way I understand that part of His word, the Bible.

OUR CHURCH- ALMOST HEAVEN IN 1987

Arnold and I were quite active in our church. We were planning a big special reunion in 1987 for our active youth groups and our Sunday school class. Arnold decided to author a book about the church with history and pictures of the church people and all the pastors we had had over the years. So, he authored the book, and I came up with the title, "Reflections and Recollections." There were many friends who helped him. To name a couple, John Luckton and Sandy Smith.

There were 16 states represented at the reunion. Some dear friends and church members who came from long distances were Charles and Janice Phipps and their sons Jerry, Joey, Johnny, and Jimmy. We had around 275 members. Some of our camping buddies were the Sarrett family, Lee and Jenny, and their family Ramona, Rita and Jimmy Harper, Roger and Betty Sarrett and children, Jerry, Eric, Kevin and Kelli. We took many trips with them and other church friends to our camp, to the beach a lot of times. Sometimes the pastor and his family went. My what good times our loving church family had! Arnold has been going there since he was born, and I have attended the same church since I married Arnold. We've always had a wonderful close fellowship with our church family.

In 1970, Arnold, Rita Harper, and I started a trio which became a quartet and grew into a larger musical group called the Gospel Tones. At first, we used our van in which to travel, then Red Bailey, our first tenor, bought our first tour bus. About six months later, Arnold bought a converted school bus with bunks and a kitchen. We only used it briefly, then bought our final bus from a group called the Gospel Tones in Roanoke, VA.

It was a great bus and served us well for more than twenty years. It seated eleven in the front and had a dinette, and a door leading to the bedroom. We had nine bunks. I covered the walls, front dash, doors, and other parts with blue carpet. We bought seat covers and had a small restroom with a porta potty and a dressing room with a large couch.

Karen Manning played piano and sang sometimes. Her brother Gerald Manning, sang base, then Butch Janney sang bass a while for the group. For a long time, Arnold sang bass, Red Bailey sang tenor, Rita sang soprano and played the piano, and I sang alto and was the mistress of ceremony for the Gospel Tones. Arnold was our business manager.

The musicians for the group were Jerry Neal on bass guitar, Charlie Asbury, electric guitar, Red Bailey sang tenor, Aileen Deck sang Alto, and Arnold Deck was our main bass singer. Later Duke Maynor sang and played rhythm guitar and wrote songs. When we first started out, Bill Dykes played bass guitar and sang. When Red Bailey quit, James Asbury sang tenor and played guitar.

Arnold was the head honcho of the group. He and I made arrangement with churches and community affairs. Bunny Campbell, a top-notch singer, songwriter, and musician, played with us and did solo work. He played a mean steel guitar. He had friends in Nashville who were musicians and made two excellent CDs. Also, we had Jim Fain on steel guitar and sometimes George Asbury.

We took trips clear across the country. We visited my brother George Brunk and his wife Rada in California. We sang at Camp Pendleton Marine Base in California, also in Kansas, Wyoming, Illinois, Michigan, Georgia, Virginia, Maryland, Pennsylvania, Florida, Ohio, and West Virginia. We made seven different recordings starting with LP's, cassettes, 8 tracks, and CD's.

The last two recordings we made we had gained a new lead singer. He was our pastor at the Crab Orchard Church of the Brethren, and he had sung with a good group in Maryland. His name was Maynard Baker. He, Rita, and I switched parts when they fit our voices. I wrote several songs and had one published called, "The Reason Why." We recorded it. Also, I wrote more songs, and some were recorded.

The Gospel Tones sang at church revivals and services. Though while we were doing all this extra work, we didn't neglect our church because we were so involved with other things there. We sang at VA hospitals, nursing homes, and community events, The Lord granted us 39 years to minister with music and the spoken word. Over the years, the men in the group have passed on over to heaven's beautiful land. The first to leave us was Red Bailey, then Jerry Neal, Charlie Asbury, then James Asbury, then lastly my dear husband, Arnold went to meet his Lord.

Occasionally, we get together with Duke Maynor who sings and plays guitar. He and his wife Brenda live in Pax, West Virginia. He writes many songs also. What a wonderful time we will have singing and playing for Jesus and our Father and the Angels in a better land.

TRACY AND OTHER LOVED ONES WHO LIVED WITH US

TRACY LYNN CROSS

I finally got the daughter I had asked God for many years before and her name is Tracy. Tracy's birth mother left three little girls and an alcoholic father. Tracy was the youngest, only six months old. Her sister, Cindy, was a little over one year older than Tracy. Their oldest sister, Susan, was 2-1/2 years older than Tracy. They lived with their father in Dayton, OH and after their mother left, their father lived with another lady, and they had two more daughters, Christine, and Teresa.

When Tracy was in the 6th grade, her father moved them to live with his mother whose name was Rachel Cross. She lived about one hundred yards from us at the time. We took the girls under our wing, took them to church, helped them celebrate Christmas, and took them for weekends at our camp on the Greenbrier River. We all loved to go to that camp. Arnold bought it when Kevin was a baby in arms. It was located on the river at Talcott near Hinton, West Virginia.

I dream quite often of that special place. We took friends to the camp and had more fun than you can imagine. We built campfires and had a large screened in back porch where we ate and could sleep a dozen or more people. The camp was on a high bank beside the river and the river flooded three or four times. After the third time, the government came in and got rid of four or five of the camps. There were six camps in total.

We had leased the land for 25 years. We had good times there and so did many of our friends. Two couples had their honeymoon there. Oh, what good memories! Much later in life, we bought three to four acres past white Sulphur Springs and later built a good five-room house on it. It is in Monongahela National Forest. It has a large bathroom and three bedrooms, large living, dining, and kitchen area. We dug a well for our water. Later we sold one of the lots to Kevin's friend, Eddie Hylton, and his wife Lori, who are dear friends of ours. Arnold's sister, Marion, who died several years ago, and her family have a camp just across the highway about a mile from our camp. All our married life, we have had camping trailers. Each one we bought was a little bit larger than the last one. We sold the last one about 10 years ago. It was getting too hard to manage as we got older.

Tracy came to live with us when she was 16 years old. She is a darling daughter. We never did legally adopt her. I wanted to but Arnold was not in agreement, so we didn't adopt. Many times, I have wished we had but anyway she could not be more our daughter then if she was our biological daughter. We have always been close to her and her daughter, Chelsea. Chelsea is one of our five grandchildren. Tracy and her husband divorced when Chelsea was three years old. Tracy has done a wonderful job raising her daughter. Tracy worked at Raleigh County job service, worked as a cook at a restaurant and many other jobs.

TAMMY CAMPBELL, TRACY, JERRY, KEVIN, AILENE, AND YVONNE AT GRADUATION PARTY

Tracy graduated from high school, and I graduated from Junior College in Beckley at the same time in the spring of 1984. I had gone to Appalachian Bible college for two years when Mark and Kevin were in grade school. I majored in Bible and minored in music.

For our graduation gift, Arnold took us and Tracy's best friend, Tammy Campbell, to a favorite place, the Kitty Hawk, Nags Head, Kill Devil Hills area to enjoy the beach and the ocean. The house we rented was close to the beach. We had a wonderful week!

I had decided I would wait until my boys grew up before I would attend the university. As it turned out, Tracy and I were going to Concord University at Athens, West Virginia at the same time. She was working on a degree in elementary art. She loved art then and still does. And she is exceptionally good at it. But she finished with a degree in Social Work, and I finished with a BS degree in Elementary Education and a BA in Psychology in 1986, and the spring of 1987. I received a Magna Cum Laud award for my college work.

Tracy was a worker in social work and later was a director at a school for troubled children called Cherry Creek shelter. I taught school as a substitute teacher and then was a supervisor at Southern High Lands Community Center program for disabled children.

I had a heart attack in February 1988 and did not work for a year. Then I worked for seven years as a parent advisor for the West Virginia School for the blind at Romney, WV but worked in a three-county area here at home. Then due to health problems, I quit work.

But I had some scholarships and Arnold pitched in for the rest. I gave him a diploma which read, "I put my wife through college."

We also helped to raise several other teenagers through the years. Jeff Campbell, who was a close friend of Mark and Kevin and held a dear place in our hearts, lived here with us for about two years.

My brother Paul Brunk and his family lived in Wilmington, Delaware as did my brother Gee Gee and at times my father. Paul and family wanted to leave the city and move to rural West Virginia. So, during the time they were making the transition, Paul's son, Paul Jr., who was in high school, came to live here for a year or more. He loved it here and we loved him. He graduated from Woodrow Wilson high school in 1978. Mark graduated in 1976, Jeff in 1977 and Kevin in 1979.

Woodrow Wilson is a big high school in Beckley where Arnold and I graduated years before. Now they have around two thousand students. So, our home was full, but happy during those years.

Richard Kincaid was a friend of Kevin's when we moved to 707 Cleveland School Rd, Beckley, West Virginia. Richard had a tough time growing up. Kevin and Richard became friends when they played basketball at Crab Orchard Elementary School. Often, we could hear the basketball hitting the hoops out on the front driveway.

Richard was forced to leave his mom and dad's home. They lived about one mile from our house when he was a little kid. I am sure he had a very unstable home life. He liked to come here and did so very often.

Richard lived in several foster homes. Later he married a girl, Becky, in Ohio. He and she had a baby boy named Dakota. At the time they were living in Crab Orchard they came to our church. I was in the room when Dakota was born. I held him and he was such a sweet little boy.

Becky would bring her clothes here to do her laundry and I got to hold Dakota a lot and rock him. Becky and Richard had him dedicated to the Lord one Sunday morning at our church. They asked Arnold and me to be Dakota's godparents, which we agreed to eagerly.

Richard got a job briefly in the coal mines. Then they left here and went back to where they used to live. When Richard was in the military, he started drinking and gambling. He had been in prison several times before he was married, and I kept up my correspondence with him. One day he called me and said he had given his heart to Jesus. I was so happy because we had talked about that quite a bit. He authored several beautiful poems which I still have. Richard was with Becky and Dakota for several years.

He began driving a big truck across country and he did very well. But one day Becky called and said he did not come home when it was expected. They, the three of them, would come here every now and then. We had a big pool in the backyard for mostly the grandchildren. She thought he had come here, but he had not.

Months later his brother, who lives in this area, called us with some shocking news. He said Richard had been living in a tent near Appalachian Bible College and he had gone to the highway to a little store. It was raining and someone hit him with a car. It was a hit and run. Richard had many injuries and was in the hospital in Charleston about sixty miles from here. He was on life support.

Arnold, Tracy, and I went there as quickly as we could. The nurse told us he was unconscious and wouldn't hear anything. We said but hearing is the last thing to go, and we wanted to go to him. We went into his room anyway. He looked so pitiful with broken legs, one arm, and his back. He had one arm bandaged up, so we took turns rubbing his uninjured arm and talking to him as if he could hear us. We were there about 3 hours.

Then I began to feel like I should sing to him. I said, "Richard this is Arnold, Aileen and Tracy and we love you and so does God and Jesus." As I began to sing Christian hymns, Arnold and Tracy watched the monitors go wild. I felt a tiny tug on my hand, so I knew he was hearing. He made no other motions when I sang 3 or 4 old songs he would recognize.

The nurse came back in and said they needed to take him off life support. We left shortly after that. We had been singing and praying and I know we got through to him. They took life support away and he died the next day. I know he went to Jesus, and we will see him again someday.

They cremated him and I gave Becky a vase for his ashes. We had a memorial service here at our house. One poem Richard wrote is titled, "His Back was Against the Wall." I still have it with my poems and others. I have included his poem titled, "Worn."

RICHARD KINCAID'S POEM - WRITTEN IN PRISON

WORN

I'm tired, I'm worn
My heart is heavy
From the work it takes
To keep on breathing,
I've made mistakes,
I've let my hope fail,
My soul feels crushed
By the weight of this world

And I know that you can give me rest
So, I cry out with all that I have left.

Let me see redemption win,
Let me know the struggle ends.
That you can mend a heart
That's frail and torn.
I wanna know a song can rise
From the ashes of a broken life.
And all that's dead inside can be reborn
Because I'm worn.

I know I need to lift my eyes up
But I am two weak.
Life just won't let up.
And I know that you can give me rest.
So, I cry out with all that I have left.

Let me see redemption win.
Let me know the struggle ends.
That you can mend a heart
That's frail and torn.
I want to know a song can rise
Even from a heart that's worn!

KEVIN'S LETTER TO BEST FRIEND, GREG

Mark made friends with Timmy (Tim) Murray who was Mark's age and lived on Old Eccles Rd. Kevin and Tim's brother Carl was Kevin's age and they went to the same school. They remained friends all their lives. Mark had another friend named David Smith, and they are still good friends.

Kevin's best friend, Greg Rodgers, died about 10 years ago of a massive heart attack. Greg's Dad had died earlier of the same thing. They owned an excavating company with all the heavy equipment that went with it. Sometimes Greg would bring a piece of heavy equipment over here to move something.

Greg's death at only 50 years of age affected Kevin deeply. Kevin wrote the sweetest epitaph I have ever read about all the things they had done together. Trips to skiing, mountain climbing, camping, hunting, and fishing were part of the things they enjoyed doing together. We sent it to the Guidepost, but they didn't accept it. Greg had two children, Shane and Emily and Kevin wrote things to Greg saying he would be a substitute Dad for them because he knew that is what Greg would do if it had been Kevin who had died. And he has kept his word along with his wife's Debbie's help. He placed the letter in Greg's casket.

This letter was read at the memorial for Greg and Kevin placed it in his coffin.

To Greg,

This is not goodbye. I have a few things to say before we meet again with the Lord Jesus, our savior.

You and I have always known that if either of us had a problem and troubles with anything, we would be there to help each other. That's a connection not many people have these days or maybe have never had. I will always cherish the thousands of hours we spent riding dirt bikes, water skiing, snow skiing, caving, camping and trips together. And all the time we spent working on trucks, boats and vehicles together. We also spent many nights and days just hanging out and never getting angry or quarrelling with each other.

Then our children came along into our lives, and we've been enjoying taking them out and watching them have fun just like we did. I know if something would have happened to me you would be there for my children. So now, you know, I'm here for Emily and Shane. I believe our kids recognize how important our friendship has been. I believe that this has been instilled within them because of our friendship. And after all, that's what friendship is all about. I will always be your friend,

Kevin

MY PROPHETIC DREAM
ABOUT OUR NEW HOUSE

One night I had a lovely dream which I thought was from the Lord Jesus. We were faithful Christians who attended the Church of the Brethren at Crab Orchard where Arnold and I were married. Mark became a follower of Jesus at the age of 8 1/2 years. Kevin became a Christian when he was nine. He attended a Good News Club at Carl and Timmy Murray's where their sister Rita held those clubs for children. They both attended and baptized at our church at Crab Orchard until they were married and had children. They now go to the Oak Grove Christian Church about a mile from where we now live.

Going back to my dream, I dreamed that Arnold and I were walking hand in hand in a lovely field. There was land around us with pretty woods, ravines, a creek, and a white house at the top of the hill near the highway.

I awoke and heard a voice that said very clearly, "You are going to have a white house on a hill with a lot of land." I knew it was the voice of God speaking.

The next day we were visiting an elderly lady, Aunt Pearl, who was sick. Arnold asked her if she knew of any place for sale - a house with at least fifty acres. She said she had heard that the

Golden and Elsie Meadows place was up for sale.

We left Aunt Pearl's house and drove a couple of miles to the place Aunt Pearl had talked about. Arnold and I went to that house, but no one was there. It looked deserted. We backed out of the driveway and started home. For some reason, I looked back and saw that a lady had driven up to the house and gone inside.

We turned around and went back to the house. Arnold knocked on the door and this time someone came to the door. Arnold asked the lady if her place was for sale. She looked puzzled, but answered, "Yes, it is, but I just decided yesterday to sell it. I haven't even told my children about it."

She asked Arnold if we wanted to look the place over. Arnold said "yes," so we took a tour of the inside. It had three bedrooms and two baths, no steps to go up and down in the front. It was a nice house with huge windows across from each other in the dining and living rooms. We walked down past the barn to the big field.

As we started walking back to the house, I realized we were walking uphill. It dawned on me that the dream I had experienced was exactly like this. I said to Arnold, "There is the white house on a hill and here is all this land. That voice that spoke to me must have been our Heavenly Father." That prophetic dream turned out to be true! We bought Elsie's house and land and moved into the house during the summer of 1971.

Later, we remodeled the house. Mark was heavily involved in the building industry at the time and put vinyl siding and new windows in our ever-improving home. We built a TV room, closet, hall, and a bathroom out of the garage. We added a new 2-car garage that was attached to the house.

About three years ago, I got an idea to name our place. Since we have always had horses and Madison not only rode horses, but she had been featured in rodeos, I wanted our placed to be called a ranch with a sign up over the barnyard gate. I told Jim Campbell, who is a talented man involved in the building business for years, about what I was thinking.

Jim drew up a plan. I told him I wanted something that honors the contributions of the men in the family. I came up with the name, "3-D Ranch," considering that Arnold, Mark and Kevin were the three Deck men who ran the place. Jim built a beautiful archway that Mark and Kevin mounted over the barnyard gate. Our ranch is now called the "3-D Ranch, LLC."

The wonderful thing about this place is that five families live on the property. There is so much land and trees that no one can see each other's house! Of course, I still live in the main house, which is situated near the highway, but I still have a big yard. There is quite a lot of space between the house and the road. Our driveway is paved and there is a big apron of blacktop in front of the double garage.

Jehovah God, our wonderful father, wants good things for his children. He has taken loving care of Arnold and me and our wonderful family. Mark and Janet live in the wooded area of the ranch in a three-story house. Kevin, Debbie, and the children live across the highway from me in the southwest part of the land. There are thirteen acres across the highway, and they live in a three-bedroom home with a big garage and over seven acres.

Chelsea lives in a new mobile home that is situated just past the main house on the northwest part of the land. She has a wonderful dog named Katya. Chelsea always stays quite busy.

Corey, Mindy, Maddy and Samuel live down on the edge of the big field. The have a beautiful double-wide home and have beautiful scenery looking out of every window.

My family all come here for Christmas, and we celebrate their birthdays here. It is such a thrill to my heart that we could give land to our children and grandchildren. They all had the land surveyed and each one has from four to seven acres except for Chelsea, who only wanted a half-acre of land. Tracy lives in her own home about one and one-half miles from the ranch.

My children and grandchildren are so good to me. They are always doing things for me that I can no longer do. We have a wonderful Heavenly Father who loves us so much and wants what is best for us.

MY SIBLINGS

RONALD, JERRY, YVONNE,
DIANA, AND LINDA
STOVER

Iris Yvonne (Brunk) Stover

My dear sister-mom, Yvonne, and husband Jerry Stover had four children, three girls (Diana, Linda, and Debbie) and one son they named Ronald. The three Stover girls went to their Church College in Anderson, Indiana, graduated and worked as teachers and Hospice Administrators. They all eventually settled in Indiana. Linda Kay married Paul Hart, a veterinarian. They live in Greenfield, Indiana. While living in Lansing, Michigan, Paul had his own veterinary hospital.

Yvonne and Jerry Stover lived in several places, but they ended up buying their first house in Beckley, sold it, and built another in Beckley. Yvonne was the oldest one in our family. She was a truly dedicated Child of God, attending the first Church of God most of her married life. She was a person of great faith. She and Jerry moved to Florida when he retired. Yvonne had taught school for several years in Fayette and Raleigh County. She had attended Beckley College and Charleston University.

DEBBIE, LINDA,
DIANA STOVER

Ronald married Nancy Reiser and they had an infant son who died at birth, then three daughters, Becky, Teresa, and Donna. They settled in Virginia Beach, Virginia. But Donna is living near Beckley now. Sadly, Ronald passed on to Jesus in 2020. All these children are real Christians as Yvonne taught them to be.

Yvonne developed brain cancer in 1995 and they had to remove her right eye. While in Florida, she got worse, and they came back to Beckley. Sadly, my lovely sister-mom passed on to her wonderful Jesus on May 3rd, 1996, at the age of seventy-five. She was an inspiration to everyone. Her husband, Jerry lived on 6 to 8 years before he left for heaven. He was so good to me the nine years of my childhood that I lived with them in their charming home in Crab Orchard.

When Yvonne died, I asked God to give me some of her abundant faith just like Elisha and Elijah. And it seems to me, God did give me more faith. I do not know if it was any of Yvonne's or not, but it does seem that I have a greater faith now. All I really know is God is always with us; He said, "I will never leave you nor forsake you."

Well, there have been many wonderful things in my journey

through life. But there have also been heartaches. But through it all, our family's faith in God has kept us on the straight and narrow path. He has been with us all the way 'Through It All" as the song says.

Ruth Wilma (Brunk) Turner

BRENDA CAROL TURNER

The first one in our family to leave for her heavenly home was Wilma and Herbert's youngest daughter, Brenda Carol, who died from encephalitis when she was 12 years old. She died on March 10th, 1959. She would have been 13 years old on March 22nd, 1959. An ambulance crew transported her to a Jackson, MI hospital. After that, Brenda was taken to the University of Michigan hospital in Ann Arbor. She was a sweet little girl and had already accepted Jesus as her savior.

They lived on Chapin St in Jackson, Michigan after moving from West Virginia in 1952. Herbert took a job at Goodyear and Wilma worked for an electrical company until she enrolled in the school of cosmetology where she got her cosmetology license. Herbert built her a nice beauty shop downstairs in their new home on Spencer drive in Jackson.

Herbert and Wilma went to Florida when they retired and bought a nice house in the Villages at Lady Lake, Florida. Wilma spent 10 to 12 years battling Alzheimer's, which we all know is a terrible disease of the brain. However, Wilma continued to fight and worked at her beauty shop in Michigan and then went to work at another beauty shop in the Villages for several years.

PATTY, LEISA, RICH, HERBERT, JOY AND WILMA

Later, as Wilma got worse, their daughter Joy, who lived in Ann Arbor, Michigan and had her own business of interior design, went to Florida, and helped them pack to move back to Michigan. Joy had some employees of a company that included her business, build a beautiful apartment upstairs in the big house she owned, and they moved into the main part of the house. Joy moved into the new upstairs apartment.

Wilma's condition worsened and she had to go to the hospital several times partly because of a urinary tract infection and other things. She had narcolepsy which later turned into cataplexy. If she got overly excited or emotional, she would just fall to the floor.

She was a very patient and kind person. She devoted time and money to Child Evangelism. Wilma and Herbert had two grandchildren, a grandson, Rich and a granddaughter, Amy Carol. Amy and Rich are Joy's children and live in Ann Arbor.

Wilma died on November 27, 2008. Herbert died when he was 93 years of age. Herbert and Wilma Turner are buried in a cemetery in Jackson, Michigan.

GEORGE AND
RADA BRUNK

George Griffith Brunk

Gee Gee and his first wife, Rada, who had died several years prior in 1996, had nine children. They had previously lived in Wilmington DE and then Lansing, Michigan. They moved the family out to California in 1964 because of the increased job opportunities and the university system for the children. Arnold and I went out to California for Rada's funeral in 1996. She was a terrific woman and mother. They had five boys and four girls. The oldest boy was David followed by the oldest girl Nancy. Then along came Larry, Lonnie, Kathleen, Christine, Pat, Donna and finally Keith. Except for Nancy who lives in Michigan with her husband Gary Hein, all the children still live in the Southern California area. (See photo of Gee Gee's family in Appendix).

In the spring of 2015, I felt the need to see my brother Gee Gee in Homeland, California. As Arnold and I kept talking about it, Arnold didn't want me to go alone, and his dialysis schedule prevented him from travelling. My niece, Debbie Stover offered to go to California with me. Arnold drove me to meet Debbie and her husband, Jerry Pittman halfway between Beckley and Indianapolis. When we left Indianapolis airport the next day, it was 14 degrees.

When we arrived at Los Angeles airport it was in the eighties. Gee Gee's son, Lon and his wife, Trudy picked us up at the airport. They are an exceptional couple. They took us to Gee Gee and Lise's home in Homeland, California.

Gee Gee built his beautiful home with the help of his sons and daughters, their spouses, and grandchildren. Gee Gee was a California state-licensed general contractor who owned a successful residential and commercial contracting business for many years. During his working career, he worked on ships, bridges, houses, and office buildings. Gee Gee was a jack-of-all-trades and a master of many of them.

When we visited him, Gee Gee was not in good health. Gee Gee was almost ninety years old, his health was failing, and he was in hospice care. We spent a wonderful week together and I went to dinner with Gee Gee's wife, Lise, a wonderful lady. I think all or many of this very loving, sweet family are Christian. A wonderful reunion awaits us someday. Sadly, we lost Gee Gee on April 14, 2015.

Paul Sidney Brunk

My youngest brother, Paul Brunk, never had good health. He was what they used to call a "blue baby" and did not have good circulation. He married a woman named Joan Lewis in Delaware. She already had two girls, Linda, and Mary. Linda and her husband, Jimmy See, moved to West Virginia, and bought a farm, a beautiful place in Monroe County. Jimmy was killed because of a four-wheeler wreck on his farm. Linda died at an early age of a heart problem. Their children still live on or near their farm. Mary lives in Lewiston, PA.

Paul had circulation problems and a bad heart. After they moved from Wilmington, Delaware to Beckley, West Virginia, he drove a Ready-Mix truck for a cement company in Beckley WV. In fact, he delivered concrete for the famous New River Gorge Bridge project.

Paul and Joan had five children, all born in Delaware but most living in West Virginia now. They love West Virginia and their church here. Paul had an operation on his legs to restore his circulation. About one year later he had a heart attack. Our darling clown passed away and went to heaven on May 7, 1980.

The following picture is of Paul Jr., his Debbie and children Cristen, Ryan, and Matt.

Joan lived on about seven more years and married again

but continued to live in the home they bought when they moved here. Just two years later, Joan died, and she was buried, as is Paul, and our dad, in the Pax Community Cemetery.

The children of Paul and Joan are Lorraine, Paul Jr., Joy, and Paula Aileen and Cindy. Linda's sister, Mary Iannone lives in Lewistown PA.

Patricia Ann Brunk

Our mutual life experiences have created a special bond with my sister Patricia Ann (Brunk) Lively. We share our deep affection for family, faith, and music. Patty was born on June 23, 1933, and married Melvin Lively at the 1st Church of the Nazarene in Jackson, Michigan on June 6, 1959. Their two children, Leisa, and Gary, live in Michigan. Patty worked at Michigan Bell Telephone Co. as an operator and the last fifteen years as an Executive Secretary. Melvin retired from Consumer's Power in 1987. Patty and Melvin were coordinators of a gospel singing group called "The Gospel Lights." Melvin played bass guitar and Patty was the lead singer and MC for the group. Daughter Leisa often joined Patty for duets and Leisa and Gary were members of the church chorale.

LEISA, GARY, MEL AND PATTY LIVELY

Patty is a song writer, poet, and an author. Several of her songs were professionally recorded by her group and they recorded two albums. She is also the author of three books including, "Patty's Promises," an autobiography published in 2001. Patty and Melvin continue to live in Michigan.

MORE ABOUT OUR CHILDREN

Mark, Kevin, Jeff, and Paul Jr. - Diver Training

Mark, Kevin, Jeff, and Paul Jr. have done many things. They worked hard and they played hard. Kevin and Jeff had been dreaming of going to Texas and learning to become deep sea divers. They left West Virginia doubling on a motorcycle in March of 1981 for Houston, Texas.

They ended up staying at one of Arnold's cousins' homes in Houston, Texas. Richard and Madeline Gallimore were wonderful hosts to them. Kevin and Jeff paid for their keep by working around the home and cleaning the pool and various other jobs.

The training to become divers was intricate and demanding. They crowded a year or more into six months of training. They went to school during the day, worked at security jobs at night, and only slept 4 hours each night. But they kept on going and worked for Solus Ocean Company, living on a ship, and working on oil rigs and underwater bridges.

But divers can't subject their bodies to constant water pressure. They worked as divers for about five years. Mark went to Houston and worked in construction. Back here in West Virginia, he was a foreman of constructing large estates on the Canyon Rim (New River Canyon). This was the epitome of nice homes in our area.

Then all three of them ended up in the state of Wyoming for eight years.

Kevin and Debbie. After their wedding, Kevin and Debbie traveled to Lovelock, Nevada where Kevin worked in a gold mine. He had previously worked at a gold mine in Colorado. Debbie worked at the trailer park store. Mark and Janet moved to Wyoming after Jeff went there. Mark and Janet bought a nice house and Mark worked at the Shoshone Coal Mine. Their only child, Corey Dean Deck was born there in Wyoming on October 23, 1989.

Mark injured his foot and was off work for a year when his horse dragged him while his foot was still in the stirrup. It twisted his knee badly and, after surgery and therapy in Laramie, WY, knee mended well. Jeff and his wife, Kerensa had their first child, Cody, and then another boy later, named Caleb. Kevin and Debbie bought a nice house in Hanna, Wyoming where Mark and Janet lived.

Kevin was an electrician in the Shoshone Coal Mine for many years. Kevin and Debbie had their first child named Kara Dawn, and when she was about three years old, their second child, Chase Woodrow was born in Laramie, WY. Kara was born with several birth problems and went through school as a special education student. She graduated and has worked in the Kroger deli department for eleven years.

During the years, the boys lived in Wyoming, Arnold and I traveled to Wyoming a couple of times a year. I even went to the Wyoming Board of Education, took tests, and taught school there for several months. The three guys and families always came home for Christmas. Every time they left, or we left Wyoming, I could not keep from crying, but it was always short-lived.

Kevin invented a critical safety feature for the mines. The superintendent wanted Kevin to go to Germany to teach them how to make the part. He also traveled to several countries. Each part of the safety feature for the miners cost $1 million dollars.
The mines purchased twenty-one of these and they are still operational in many mines in the area.

One time Arnold, Kevin, Jeff, and I camped high in the Rocky Mountains at the 11,000-foot level so the men could hunt and fish. We were there 10 days. I wrote a little book about it.

Arnold loved to travel as I did. We took our boys and traveled all over the United States and Canada. We traveled in all the states except Hawaii. We have friends and relatives all over the country and we have visited many of them and we have seen interesting sights.

When Tracy was living with us, she had the opportunity to travel with us especially when we were in the singing and musical Gospel Tones. We had a good used Trailways bus and traveled and performed. We made seven recordings at good recording studios. God has granted us an interesting life.

Our boys, Mark and Kevin, moved back to West Virginia so Debbie could take care of her dear mother who was sick. Kevin and family moved back first and later Mark, Janet, and Corey moved back here. Mark went into the home building business with Arnold and called it "A and M Construction." They built Mark's home and Kevin and Debbie bought a doublewide and moved it on our property. "A and M Construction" went on to build several residences in our area.

Debbie's dear mother passed away two years after they moved back. Kevin and Mark both have worked in the coal mining industry. Kevin worked as an electrician and Mark had various jobs there. Mark just retired at age 62 after several years with the mines. Kevin is now travelling hours away to Williamson Mine. He and Mark work from dawn till dark cutting trees and other things when the power company came through our land and left work for them to do.

MAY I TELL YOU ABOUT MY GRANDCHILDREN?

Mark and Janet's only child is Corey Dean Deck. He was born in Rawlins, Wyoming when they lived at Hannah, Wyoming. Corey was born October 23rd, 1989. He was adorable. He still is. Mark and Janet moved back here to West Virginia when Corey was a baby. He was so cute. When he was two years old or so, Arnold and I took our John boat down to our pond and let him row the boat.

We have a little creek rippling down through the woods and Cory and I put on boots and went trampling down through the little creek. That was so precious! Picking wildflowers to take to his Mommy was something else he enjoyed. He loved for Papa to take him riding on the tractor. Oftentimes the whole family built a big bonfire and had a sleigh riding party using sleds and inner tubes. We all had fun as a family in the summer and the winter.

Once, when Corey was about nine years old, he was riding in a four-wheeler up the steep road leading to the highway. It was winter and the road was icy. He had a bad wreck when the 4-wheeler went over the steep hill. But even though he was a little kid, he gave credit to God's angels for saving his life. He told me later that the handlebars were on each side of his shoulders, keeping the weight of the four-wheeler off his body. He has always been quick to give God glory for things in life. Corey accepted Jesus when we were riding our van up to our camp at Sherwood Lake, ninety-two miles away.

Kevin and Debbie had three children. Kara Dawn was born in Rawlings, Wyoming. She was born with birth problems which slowed her development. She has a hearing problem, but with hearing aids she can communicate fine. She had to follow the special education program all through school but passed her Drivers Ed class. Kara has been employed for more than 11 years at a local Kroger store in the deli department. She is a very capable and respected employee. She helps her mother teach children's classes at Oak Grove Christian Church.

Chase Woodrow is Kevin and Debbie's second child. He was born in Laramie, Wyoming, on September 7th, 1994. He was such a cute little boy. When he was 15 years old, he contracted a dreaded disease. He was in Women's and Children's Hospital in Charleston West Virginia in the ICU for about 2 weeks. They diagnosed him as having encephalitis. Our niece, Brenda Turner, died of encephalitis when she was almost 13 years old. We were all worried about Chase.

One night, about 3:00 AM, the Lord Jesus woke me up and told me we needed to get a minister or someone to anoint him with oil in the name of the Lord and the prayer of faith would save the sick. This scripture can be found in James 5:14. It says, "is any sick among you? Let him call for the elders of the church, and let them pray over him, anointing him with oil in the name of the Lord. And the prayer of faith will save the sick, and the Lord will raise him up. And if he has committed any sins, he will be forgiven."

Since we didn't have a pastor at this time, I tried calling several pastors I knew but none of them could go to Charleston so I called our Deacon, Jim Campbell, a fine man, and asked him if he would do it. He said "yes." Jim Campbell, and his wife Sue, went to Charleston. Arnold and I were on our way there, as well.

When we got there, Debbie and her Christian friends and family were in a waiting room. The staff wouldn't let but two people in the ICU with Chase, so Kevin was in there with him, and Jim went in. Jim read the scripture of James 5:14 and then made the sign of the cross with oil on Chase's forehead. Chase was unconscious at the time. Kevin had grown up in our church and knew that scripture and had seen the anointing service performed many times. While they were there with Chase, all of us in the waiting room formed a circle and prayed.

Soon, Arnold I went in to see Chase. He awoke and said, "I'm hungry. Can someone bring me some food?" A nurse came and brought him some 7UP and Jell-O. Chase said, "No, I want some real food." So, they brought him a meal of chicken, mashed potatoes, and the whole works. He ate like a starving person. He had regained consciousness, ate a full meal, and seemed like his old self again. We all were full of joy and thankfulness. It was two days later that he was at home. Chase is an electrical technician at a local electrical company called,

Lowe Brothers Electrical.

While he was in the hospital, Chase's dog Spunky ran away and we couldn't find him. I and others were praying for him to come home. I really don't remember if Spunky came home the day Chase did, or a day or two later, but he did come back. Another answered prayer. God is so good! He genuinely cares about people and our little animals.

Kevin and Debbie's last child was born in Beckley, West Virginia on February 18th, 2001. Her name is Madison Rose. She is now a student at a university in Murray, Kentucky. She has always been a four-plus point student and plans to be a veterinarian, working with large animals. She is particularly fond of horses. She has been performing in rodeos since the age of twelve. She is a good singer, leading praise and worship and singing specials at Oak Grove Christian Church.

She sang the Star-Spangled Banner and carried the flag at several rodeos. She has competed at the four nationals' rodeos, two in Wyoming, one in Iowa and one in Missouri.

Our fifth grandchild is Chelsea Lynn Hicks. Chelsea was born in a Beckley hospital on April 3rd, 1996. She is our daughter Tracy's only child. Tracy and Chelsea's dad Mike Hicks divorced when Chelsea was three years old.

She graduated from Woodrow Wilson high school and has attended College in Beckley and Concord college where Tracy and I graduated. She plans to go back and get her degree in social work. Chelsea is an extremely sweet 26-year-old and is presently employed by a realty company doing title searches. She had a job at one time with Visiting Angels. All my grandchildren love helping people. I am so proud of all of them.

Now, we have our first great-grandson, Samuel Dean Deck born in Beckley on July 24th, 2019, to our grandson Corey and his wife Melinda (Mindy). He is such a precious, beautiful baby full of life. He has been walking for quite a while and he runs more than he walks. He already has a mouth full of teeth and has light brown hair and blue eyes. His hair is curly, and Mindy is debating about getting it cut.

Mindy is such a great cook. She has a daughter, a teenager from a previous marriage. She is about 13 years old, and her name is Madison (Maddy). Her mom has home schooled her all the time even before the COVID virus showed up. Corey and Mindy are happy. They love the beach. In fact, they love it so much that they had their wedding at the beach.

ANOTHER PROPHETIC DREAM: THE WELL (1998)

After we moved to the place where we currently live, I had dreamed about what my Dear Lord said, that we would have a White House on a hill with land. We were so happy here. We moved here on March 8th, 1971.

Arnold and the boys worked so hard to get the place in order. They had to cut brush, clean up a trash pile, work on the barn, and many other duties. They also had to kill copperhead snakes and thankfully there are no more of them now.

We have a lovely pond down in a ravine over the hill from the house. This was our water supply for many years. The water was piped up to the basement where we had our own treatment system. In the summer, the water turned a reddish color. I couldn't wash clothes in it so in summer I went to the laundromat.

We decided to dig a well. We had a well digging crew come and dig it and put in the casing and all the parts required of a well. Again, I had a very prophetic dream. Arnold was working out of town at the time, and I called and told him about my dream. I dreamed that a voice said to me "they will hit water at 186 feet."

They finished the digging. The head man said they didn't hit a gusher of water but maybe after it's settled there would be more water. We piped water through the kitchen sink and Arnold and the boys would go to Momaw Deck's and fill 50-gallon tanks with good drinking water. They did that for several years. Finally, the city put in city water. Hallelujah!

One day Jeff Campbell, who was living here at the time, came into the kitchen where I was working, and Jeff said he was going to measure down to the water in the well. He tied a cord around a "pop" bottle then let it go down until he knew it hit water because it gurgled. He pulled it up, laid it out in the long side driveway and preceded to measure the cord.

Jeff had already had one year of College in Charleston and had been living with us for more than a year. He had lived across from our church with his mother. He was 13 years old when she died. His dad did not live with them for several years. A year after his mother died, his dad died. Jeff loved to come to our house because we had a farm with cattle and horses and with a wooded area. He, Mark, and Kevin would build cabins in the woods and a two-story treehouse in a big oak tree near our house. Our house always felt like home to Jeff and the three boys have been close as brothers ever since.

But I digress. Let me get back to that dream. After measuring the cord, Jeff came into the kitchen grinning. He said, "How many feet do you think it is?"

I said, "I don't know, how much?"

He said, "186 feet."

I said "Can you believe it? It's true! They hit water at 186 feet just like I heard The Voice say in my dream!" After I had experienced two prophetic dreams, Arnold and I knew this place was surely meant for us to have. As of this writing, we have lived here fifty years. We all have been tremendously happy here. We now call it the 3-D Ranch, LLC and all the children and grandchildren live here on the same property. Praise the Lord for all His goodness to us.

YVONNE'S FINAL POEM

"Blinded by His Glory"

After Yvonne and Jerry came back to live in Beckley, WV from their home at Orange Blossom Gardens in Florida, Jerry had been noticing unusual symptoms that suggested that cancer in Yvonne's eye was not all there was to it. They decided to come back to their home in Beckley.

Herbert and Wilma decided to come back with them. And it was good that they did. Yvonne had seizures on the way home. After consulting a doctor who specializes in cancer, they discovered that Yvonne also had brain cancer. Of course, we were all so distressed. She was in the hospital on painkilling drugs and steroids. The doctor asked Jerry what kind of pain medication she had been on. He told the doctor nothing but Tylenol. She surely endured too much pain and suffering.

One day I called her at the hospital, and she told me she had a poem running through her mind but could not remember all of it. She asked me if I would finish it for her. Yvonne wrote the first four lines and then I finished it the way I thought she would have wanted it done.

The final poem, "Blinded by His Glory," contains her first four lines but have also included some of her last thoughts. I am sure God gave both of us the words He wanted her to write.

"Oh, Ailene. It is so wonderful? I feel the power of God so real. How wonderful! I hate to leave my loved ones here, but God will take care of them, and I'll see them all in a better place."

I again said, "We'd better hang up honey, you're tired." She said very adamantly, "No- I've got more to say. I love that song Mom loved so well. "I Come to the Garden Alone." We said some of the words together, And He walks with me, and He talks with me."

I said, "Do you want that song at your funeral?"

She said, "Yes, that's what I have been trying to think about- it keeps slipping away."

I asked her, "Do you want the choir to sing it or someone else?

She said, "Whatever you want to do, however you want to do it, is OK by me."

I struggled but answered, "OK."

She said God has been with me through it all. We began to sing, "Through It All."

"Through It All, Through It all, I've learned to trust in Jesus, I've learned to trust in God, Through It All."

Yvonne switched to her alto voice and began to sing, "Through It All, I've learned to depend upon his Word!"

She continued, "I wanted to write more songs and poems."

I told her that, "Jarrett will finish your book of poems and I will find your songs and Bunny and I will put music to them, and I promise you they will be sung."

She said, "Oh, thank you!" I keep trying to write a song called, "Blinded by His Glory," but can't get it together."

I said, "Do you want me to help you?"

Yvonne said, "Yes, please do," and begun saying the first four lines of the poem.

> The love kept flowing and flowing
> and His Glory kept glowing & glowing.
> I see His face more clearly now
> as I prepare to cross the brow

(At this point, Yvonne asked that I finish the poem)

> That leads me up to Zion's hill
> Where I'll forever do His Will.
> Oh, how glorious will be my crossing-
> As the billows keep on tossing
> His hand is guiding all the way,
> and gives me strength from day to day.

He'll hold me closely to His breast,
Until it is time for me to rest.
I want the whole wide world to know,
as I wait until it's time to go,
That serving Him has been a joy
That Satan never can destroy!

The road's been rough- the hills were steep
Sometimes I had to stop and weep
But I have promises to keep
That I'll fulfill before I sleep
God give me strength to do Thy will
and then I'll climb to Zion's hill.

Chorus

Oh, the glory that awaits,
When I see Him face to face
Glory! Glory! to His Name
Let all the earth and Heav'n proclaim!
Kneel- Oh kneel before His throne
Let Him make your heart His home.

My beloved Sister-Mother, Yvonne died on May 3, 1996. She
was 75 years old.

ARNOLD GOES TO HIS
HEAVENLY HOME

Arnold had to go into Beckley on Tuesdays, Thursdays, and Saturdays every week for dialysis. It took four hours each trip. He had been born with only one kidney that performed as it should. The blood vessels going to his kidneys were not efficient, so when he got older his urologist said he would need to be on dialysis unless he could have a transplant.

We went to a transplant team in Charleston, WV. They assessed him and concluded that since he had suffered heart attacks in the past, he was not a viable candidate for a transplant.

His first heart attack was in 1998. That was the one in which he suffered heart damage. I had begged him to go to the hospital, but he wouldn't go. Both arms were very painful. One night, about 2:00 AM, he woke me and wanted to go to the hospital. This time he did have a heart attack with heart damage.

The next time that it happened, I immediately gave him an aspirin, a nitroglycerin tablet and called an ambulance. He did have a heart attack again, but fortunately the heart received no further damage. That was a year or so after the first one. In 2000, he had a third heart attack and again I gave him an aspirin and nitroglycerin and again there was no damage. But because of those attacks, he was not a candidate for a kidney transplant. So, he began dialysis in the year 2011.

We tried home dialysis, but he thought it wasn't as effective as going to the clinic, so we gave that up and he started back with no interruption in service. He went to dialysis almost eight years. He drove himself there and back for every appointment except for one. He had determination. Both of our boys are just like him in that regard and many other respects. They do not start a project unless they think.

In the fall of 2018, Arnold was not feeling very well. He tired easily and just did not feel well. He began to have shortness of breath and it was getting increasingly difficult for him to talk. He had to stop and get his breath as he talked to me, our family, and friends.

After many struggles, he ended up in the Raleigh General Hospital, which is one of our two hospitals in Beckley. He was there for a week, and they did dialysis four times that week. I felt like he also had congestive heart failure. His hands and arms were swelling. The year was 2018 and it was in November and bitterly cold.

The staff at Raleigh General released him to come home on a Saturday evening. After he was home for a while, he began having such a tough time breathing that we called an ambulance to come over to the house. We wanted them to take him to CAMC (Charleston Area Medical Center) in Charleston, West Virginia which was a much better hospital. But the ambulance attendants said they had a ruling that patients must be taken to the closest hospital. They checked him over and gave him oxygen and then left.

The next morning, Mark and Kevin took him to CAMC. They admitted him, put him in ICU and said he was in critical condition. They began to drain fluid off his lungs. They drained more than five two-liter bottles of fluid out of his lungs. I wanted them to do dialysis on him, but the doctors said he was not able to take dialysis.

On Monday morning, Kevin called me as he had stayed the night with him. I answered the phone and Arnold tried to talk to me but didn't have enough breath to talk. I was finally able to make out the words "home and tired." I didn't know it then, but Kevin told me later he wanted to tell me goodbye.

I told Arnold that I knew he was tired, and many people were praying for him. I said, "We've been praying that God would heal you but if you really want to go home to Jesus, we all as a family give you, our blessing."

His sister Janet, some of our church people, nieces, and nephews, and of course our children, and grandchildren were there most of the time. On Thursday morning, the head doctor came in and said that Arnold's body just could not fight all the things he was going through. They placed him on life support.

We stayed by his bedside all the time. We held his hands, and his hands and arms were still very swollen. Thursday evening the doctors and the family made the difficult decision to take him off the life support but to keep giving him oxygen and pain medication. All day Friday he kept looking around the room from left to right and back and to the ceiling. I am sure he was seeing Angels!

Arnold took his final breath at 5:08 PM on November 23rd, 2018. I had been telling him all week that our 63rd anniversary was November 24th but although he fought valiantly, he could not make it to the 24th. He died peacefully and I know God's Angels took him to his heavenly home.

I miss him so much. He was such a good man who never met a stranger and would do anything for anybody. I know our reunion will be wonderful! I look forward to seeing my dear Lord Jesus, my dear husband, and my dear family.

Meanwhile my children and grandchildren, nieces and nephews have all been so kind to me. Jesus said I will never leave you alone; He is my rock, my anchor.

About six months after Arnold went home to Jesus, I knew I needed a companion. So, Tracy and the Lord arranged for me to get a darling six-month old Shih-tzu Maltese mix. She is all white and a real darling. I named her Angel, and she is the joy of my life, after Jesus and of course, my family always comes first.

APPENDIX

George G. Brunk family picnic in California – 1983

FIGURE 2 GEE GEE BRUNK

FAMILY PICNIC IN CALIFORNIA - 1983

1. Nicole Danielle Brunk
2. Jennifer Michele Brunk
3. Alisa Elaine Brunk (Denny)
4. Rada Blanche Brunk (Sharp)
5. Sandra Lee Brunk (Self)

FAVORITE PLACES

By Ailene Deck, March 12, 1986

Do you ever think about favorite places? Once upon a time, many years ago, when I was a little girl, I took my doll, Marguerite, and a book to a favorite place. That place was a little corner of a closet under a stairway. I went there often to while away time. Although I couldn't read yet, I "read" to Marguerite and then I would daydream... as I still do. And I still have some favorite places.

Right now, I am sitting in one of those favorite places... a cozy chair by my dining room window. I have spent any hours here, not because I am old or tired, but because it is here that I do my studying. I am 50 years old and in my senior year of college. I want to graduate and become a teacher. After graduate school, I want to be a child psychologist.

As I sit here learning about interesting people, places, events, and ideas, I often look out the window. The world I am reading about and the world I'm living in merge together.

Right now, as I write, there is a drama taking place out there un-der that ancient black walnut: a bright red cardinal just flew from the ground over to an apple tree by the barn gate where he and I watch two doves walking so sedately around the 'ole walnut's trunk, eating happily now and then the grains that get scattered there.

A small red headed woodpecker was just there, now he is making his way up and up, around, and around to a high branch on the tree. Here comes a friend of his and they sit there quietly, for a mo-ment, and then he flits to another branch... now he flies away... and I wonder where to?

My friends, those tall, tall trees, down in the ravine, whose branches sway in the breeze, today seem to fulfill the scripture in Psalms where David said, "the trees clap their hands for joy."
The big old white pine down in the field is having its say too, bowing to the mighty oak across the hill...
The "big field" is quiet today - no cattle there right now. I saw a deer there one day, just at the edge of the woods. Soon, there will be frisky baby calves there, frolicking about, watched over by their mommas.

That old, gnarled apple tree has seven, stubborn, dried-up Grimes Golden apples hanging there in the top branches like ancient kings sitting on their thrones. What an object lesson! They possess a rare tenacity, hanging on stubbornly through the cold winds of winter. So many precious lessons are learned from the simplicity of nature.

The pond was laced with ripples today. Usually, it is quiet. I can gauge the amount of wind we have by the ripples on her face. Last night, I went outside and listened to the frogs "sing." I love their spring serenade.

I look upward. Day before yesterday, the sky was the most bril-liant blue - totally beautiful! And the sun was so brilliant! Today, it is a light blue grey, no sunshine; not great, but not bad - Just ho-hum.

There is a beautiful piece of music wafting from the stereo and my reverie must end. I have things to do, but that reminds me…

A few days ago, Lady (my dog) and I took a walk down past the big field into the woods. There were big, tall trees, some bare, but
beautiful; some green, all bent over with snow. The snow is sever-al inches deep down there across the fence where the mountain lau-rel grows and the little creek meanders here and there. It was so quiet, so peaceful.

God was all around me, I felt Him walking with me, stopping with me to drink the beauty of His creativity, and I thought, (as I al-ways do when I am in the woods on a snowy day) about what Robert Frost (one of my favorite poets) said in his poem "Stopping by Woods On A Snowy Day":

"…but I have promises to keep, and miles to go before I sleep."

And so do I!

Written by Ailene (Brunk) Deck
March 12, 1986

"WHERE THE PURPLE IRISES BLOOM" BY KEITH BRUNK

One day I will hug my Grandma and shake my Grandpa's hand. I'll listen to their stories about living off the land.

They will tell me of their children and of their dreams so grand. About all the great adventures they had with Rex and Dan.
I'll tell them that I love them, and about how grateful that I am that their spirit still burns so bright throughout our entire clan.

KEITH BRUNK

I'll share with them my joy at seeing Ailene's wonderful smile, of the warmth and love that live in Wilma's hands, of the strength and dignity of Yvonne, and the humor of Patty Ann.

I'll tell them of the laughter I shared with their son Paul
About how hard that Gee Gee had worked, so I could meet them all.

As they share with me their wisdom, I'll memorize all I can,
I'll tell them how their children all helped make me a better man.

How they taught me about sacrifice, how to love, and lend a hand.
I know, one fine day we'll all share a beautiful piece of land,

Where I can hug my Grandma, and shake my Grandpa's hand'.

Sometimes when I am troubled and my spirit's full of gloom,
I'll dream of Grandma's hug, *where the purple irises bloom.*

FAMILY PHOTOS

Paul, Debbie, Cristen, Ryan and Matt Brunk

Paul Sydney Brunk

1916 Photo: Jack, Macil, Ronald, Grandma Martha, Donald, Mattie, Ruth & Lillian (Age 15)

Joy Turner

Patty, GG and Ailene

Sydney and George Brunk

Wilma and Yvonne

Ailene and Arnold's 50th Wedding Annivrsary

GEORGE, PATTY, AND AILENE 2010
AT PITTMAN HOUSE

DEBBIE, LINDA, DIANA STOVER

PITTMAN REUNION JULY 1997

PITTMAN REUNION JULY 2012

DOROTHY, RUTH, MATTIE, LOTTIE, LAURA

PEDIGREE CHART FOR LILY AILENE BRUNK

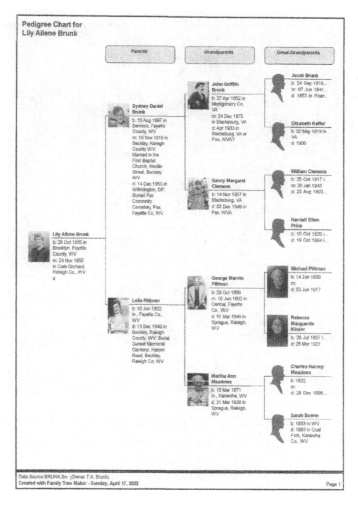

Pedigree Chart for Lily Ailene Brunk

Parents	Grandparents	Great-Grandparents

Lily Ailene Brunk
b: 28 Oct 1905 in Brooklyn, Fayette County, WV
m: 24 Nov 1955 in Crab Orchard, Raleigh Co., WV
d:

Sydney Daniel Brunk
b: 15 Aug 1897 in Dernock, Fayette County, WV
m: 15 Nov 1919 in Beckley, Raleigh County WV; Married in the First Baptist Church, Neville Street, Beckley, WV
d: 14 Dec 1955 in Wilmington, DE; Buried Pax Community Cemetery, Pax, Fayette Co, WV

John Griffith Brunk
b: 27 Apr 1852 in Montgomery Co, VA
m: 24 Dec 1875 in Blacksburg, VA
d: Apr 1933 in Blacksburg, VA or Pax, WVA?

Jacob Brunk
b: 24 Sep 1819...
m: 07 Jun 1841...
d: 1853 in Roan...

Elizabeth Keffer
b: 02 May 1819 in VA
d: 1900

Nancy Margaret Clemens
b: 14 Nov 1857 in Blacksburg, VA
d: 02 Dec 1949 in Pax, WVA

William Clemens
b: 25 Oct 1817 i...
m: 30 Jan 1843
d: 23 Aug 1903...

Harriett Ellen Price
b: 15 Oct 1820 i...
d: 19 Oct 1904 i...

Lelia Pittman
b: 10 Jun 1902 in , Fayette Co., WV
d: 13 Dec 1940 in Beckley, Raleigh County, WV; Burial Sunset Memorial Gardens, Harper Road, Beckley, Raleigh Co, WV

George Marvin Pittman
b: 29 Oct 1889
m: 10 Jun 1902 in Central, Fayette Co., WV
d: 31 Mar 1949 in Sprague, Raleigh, WV

Michael Pittman
b: 14 Jun 1830
m:
d: 03 Jun 1917

Rebecca Marguerite Kinzer
b: 28 Jul 1837 i...
d: 25 Mar 1921

Martha Ann Meadows
b: 15 Mar 1871 in , Kanawha, WV
d: 31 Mar 1938 in Sprague, Raleigh, WV

Charles Harvey Meadows
b: 1832
m:
d: 28 Dec 1898...

Sarah Boone
b: 1833 in WV
d: 1883 in Coal Fork, Kanawha Co., WV

Data Source BRUNK.ftm (Owner T.A. Brunk)
Created with Family Tree Maker - Sunday, April 17, 2022

Page 1

DOROTHY, RUTH, MATTIE, LOTTIE, LAURA

AILENE, ARNOLD, AND FAMILY

STANDING: ARNOLD, MARK, KEVIN, AND AILENE

SEATED: JANET, DEBRA (HOLDING "LADY"), TRACY

Made in the USA
Middletown, DE
22 May 2022

66039151R00163